Trackways

Fenella Flack and Rosemary Winnall

Flack Publishing

Flack Books, 23 Stourport Road, Bewdley, Worcestershire DY12 1BB, UK

www.flackbooks.weebly.com

First edition 2023

Printed in the UK by Rotary Printers (Stourport-on-Severn) Ltd, Mitton Street, Stourport-on-Severn DY13 9AA

ISBN 978-1-9163005-3-8

Foreword

Do we today use tracks walked by our pre-historic ancestors? It is very likely that our major routeways are those forged by animals and early humans. However, we know some roads are new, for instance, Bewdley's bypass. We suspect that some routes may have been lost either through neglect or by being built upon.

Rosemary Winnall and I set out to try and find those ancient trackways. We had a lot of fun in doing so and now share our findings. We suggest that some might be earlier than others. We may not be right, but you can still enjoy these routes used by people of long ago. Some trackways are main roads and some are inaccessible, but there are sections which can be enjoyed as walks.

My thanks to Rosemary for supplying the photos of the animal tracks and the one of Lodge Banks on the back cover.

Fenella Flack

Contents

Into Bewdley from the west – Map showing the range of walks

Into Bewdley from the east – Map showing the range of walks

West 1 – Henley to Bewdley – 7 ½ miles (walking) and 12 miles (by car) Page 1

West 2 – Clows Top to Bewdley – 5½ miles 13

West 3 – High Clows to Dunley – 5½ miles 28

West 4 – Far Forest to Dunley – 5 miles 39

West 5 – Buttonbridge to Dowles Brook – 2½ miles 53

A walk at Far Forest– 2¼ miles 69

Animal tracks 75

West 6 – Rock to Wharton Park – 3 miles 78

The Whitty Pear 87

West 7 – Wyre Forest Visitor Centre to Button Oak – 2¾ miles 90

West 8 – Wyre Forest Visitor Centre to Bewdley via Deasland – 8 miles 101

West 9 – Coneygreen to Bewdley via Stagborough Hill – 5 miles 110

West 10 – A circular walk from Button-oak via Kingswood – 3½ miles 117

Crossing the Severn 127

East 1 – Shatterford to
Northwood Lane –3¼ miles 130

East 2 Halls Farm to Bridewell
(inaccessible) 141

East 3 – Shatterford to
Upper Arley – 2 miles 142

East 4 – Shatterford to opposite
Hawkbatch – 2 miles 147

East 5 – Shatterford to Netherton –
4¼ miles 160

East 6 – Hoarstone to Bewdley –
1 mile 165

East 7 – Hall's Farm Lane to
Bewdley – 2 miles 168

East 8 – Two routes to
Kidderminster, one now lost 174

East 9 – Gilgal to Bewdley via
Burlish Top – 3 miles 178

East 10 – Gilgal to Bewdley via
The Brant – 3¾ miles 183

Epilogue 191

Our thanks go to Bewdley Bards, Bewdley Historical Research Group, Bewdley Library, Peter Bill, Nigel Dobson-Smyth, James Fernihough, Josh Harry, John Holloway, Barbara Hutt, Andrew Jones, Derry and Deborah Machin, Barry and Avril Maloy, Cedric Quayle, Alan Stanley, Tony Winnall, Gillian and Graham Wire, Worcestershire Archive and Archaeology Service especially for their permission to reproduce the map on p. 157 which John Broome made for the Dean and Chapter of Worcester in 1756. AND all those interesting people we met on our walks who kindly shared their knowledge about their locality.

Routes west of the river

Primary routes red
Secondary routes green

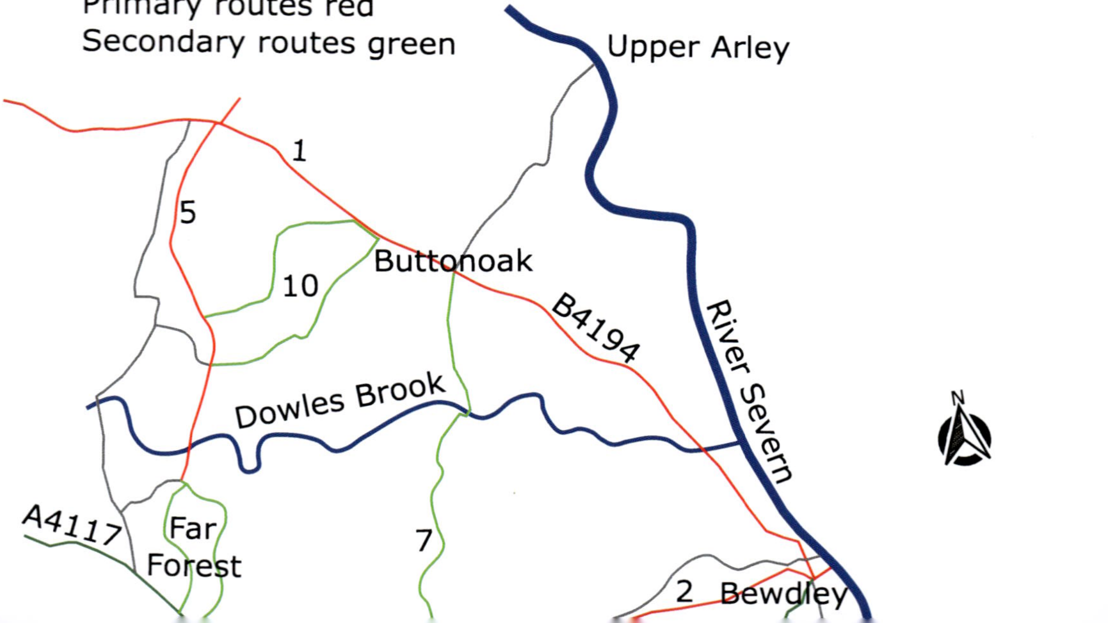

Far Forest
7
2
A456
4
8
6
2
Clows
Top
6
8
9
River Severn
Rock
3
4
Dunley

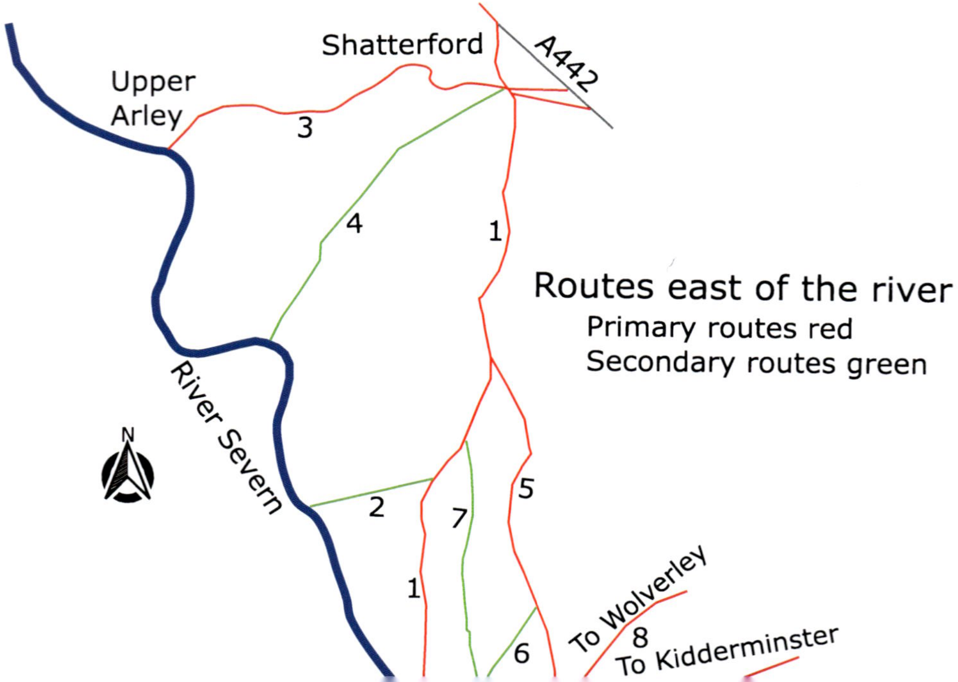
Routes east of the river
Primary routes red
Secondary routes green
Shatterford
A442
Upper
Arley
River Severn
N
1
2
3
4
5
6
7
8
1
To Wolverley
To Kidderminster

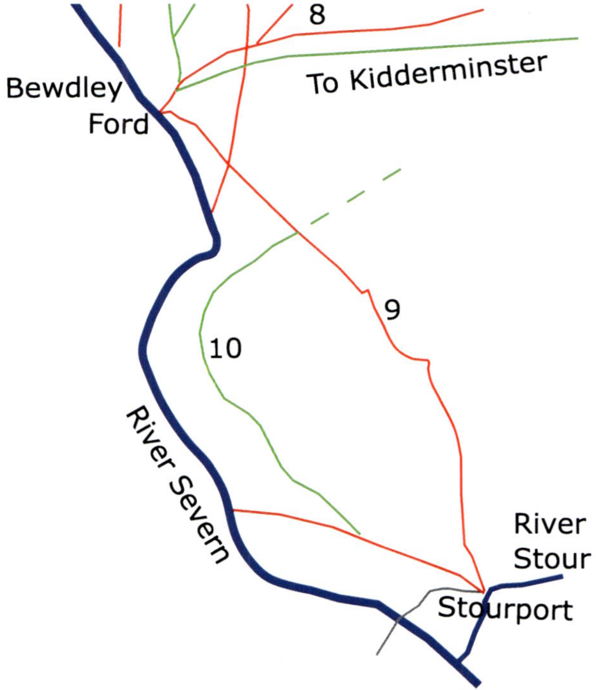
8
To Kidderminster
Bewdley
Ford
9
10
River Severn
River
Stour
Stourport

N.B. Please be aware that the routes can change over time and access may be difficult in different seasons. They were alright when we walked them!

Other local history books by Fenella Flack:

Wribbenhall just before the railway came
Bewdley The early years (out of print)
Pieces of Wyre (in two volumes)
Bewdley under the White Rose
Walking Bewdley's History
Walking Stourport's History
Walking Kidderminster's History
Death in the Severn (a novel)

Also:

Eds Brett Westwood, Peter Shirley, Rosemary Winnall and Harry Green, *The Nature of Wyre* (Pisces, 2015) – on pp. 18-19 this book explains the geology of Wyre and the surrounding area.

West 1 – Henley to Bewdley – 7 ½ miles (walking) and 12 miles (by car)

It may seem strange to begin a book on Bewdley's ancient trackways by describing a walk near Ludlow. This trackway is part of a network of prehistoric routes throughout our land. Its significance for us is that it crosses the Severn at Bewdley, thus putting this place at the busy heart of an ancient landscape.

This prehistoric way has been identified by the large number of artefacts, such as flint tools, found along its route.[1] Lily Chitty described it in 1963 and gave it the name of the Clun-Clee Ridgeway. She

---

[1] Chitty, L. F., 'The Clun-Clee Ridgeway: a prehistoric trackway across south Shropshire' in I. LL. Foster and L. Alcock (eds), *Culture and Environment: Essays in honour of Sir Cyril Fox* (London, 1963), pp. 171-192

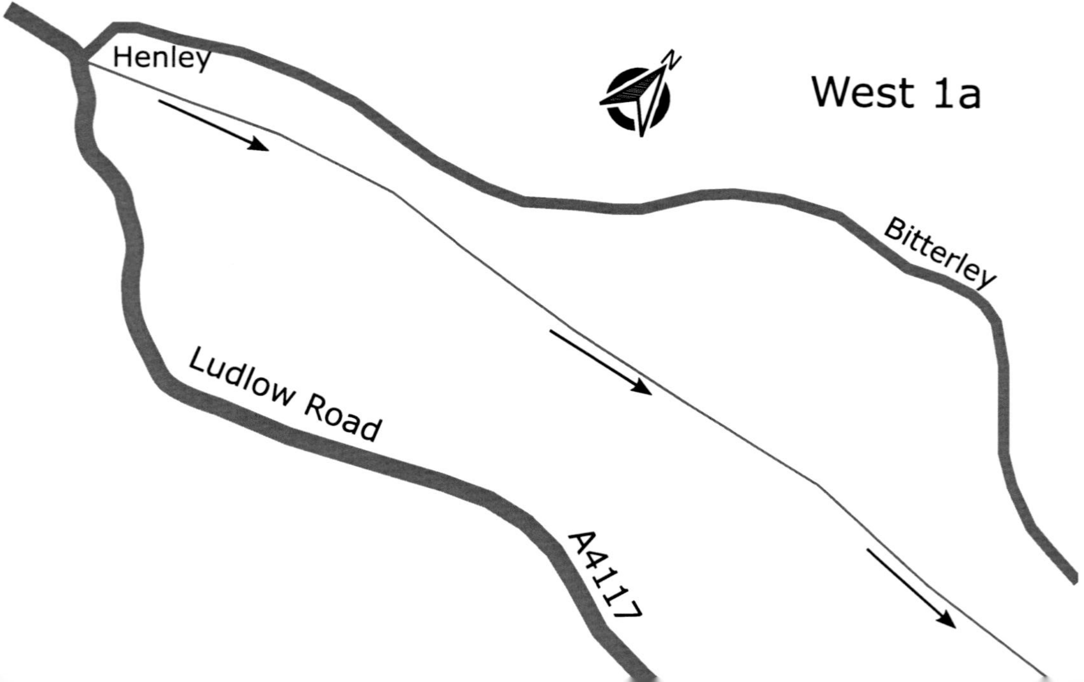

West 1a

traced it from the Kerry Hill Ridgeway in Wales to the River Severn at Bewdley.

It can be picked up east of Ludlow at Henley (SO542764) where a footpath goes northeast from the junction of the main road (A4117) and the lane marked Henley. [See Map West 1a] The route is almost a straight line and in the distance is Titterstone Clee, a landmark which must also have guided early man.

You pass through a farm called Asbatch and further on pass another called The Furlongs. Look out for hares in the fields near here. [Move on to Map West 1b] After nearly two miles, you come to a tarmacked road. Here the old routeway has been obliterated by the building of the railway and the Titterstone Incline. Turn left and after a short walk (by a bus shelter with a bench!), turn sharp right to follow the lane to Bedlam. As you cross a stream and the lane rises, you are back on the old route and as you walk up to Bedlam, you can see you are walking on a ridgeway. Ridgeways were the preferred trackways because they were more likely to be dry, whereas the valley bottoms were wooded and marshy. Also you got a better view on a ridgeway. Bedlam is said to take its name from a hospital for the mentally ill which was

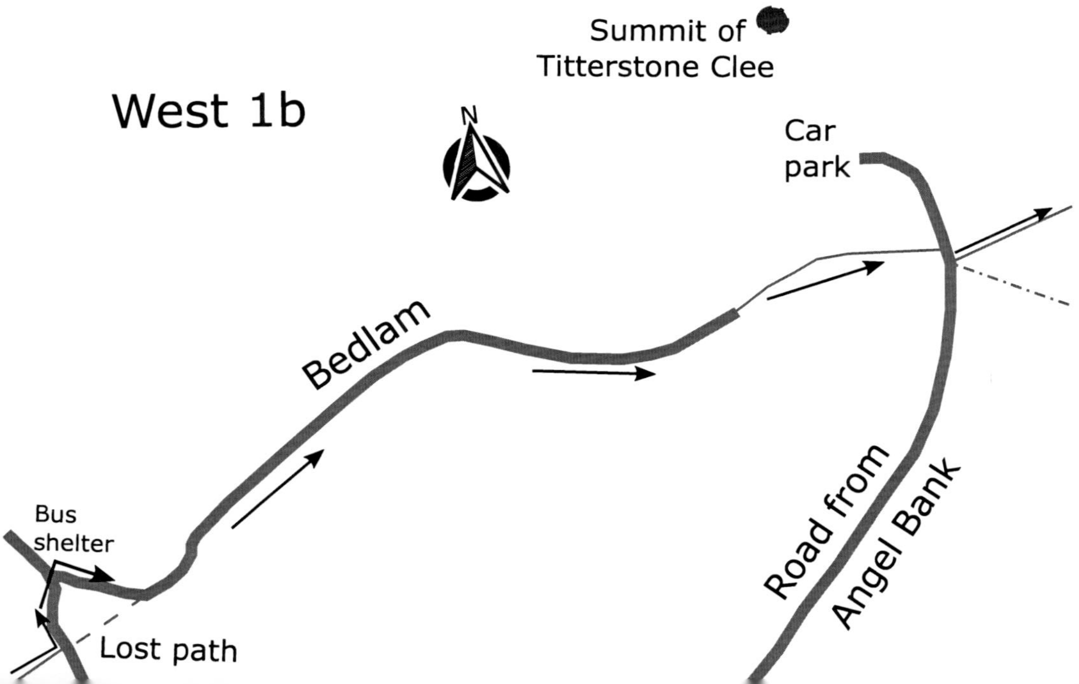
West 1b
Summit of
Titterstone Clee
N
Car
park
Bedlam
Road from
Angel Bank
Bus
shelter
Lost path

located nearby. It is a tiny place with magnificent views to the south. It is about 2 ½ miles from the start.

You are now on Titterstone Clee and can follow the tarmacked lane and then a rough trackway round its base. The vegetation is quite different up on the hillside with gorse growing on the old quarry spoil. Many different lichens may be seen on the rocks and Meadow Pipits flit across the moorland calling as they fly. A wide variety of fungi may be found amongst the short sheep-grazed turf in the autumn. When you reach the road leading to the car park and the quarry, turn right for a short distance and then take a path across the moorland heading for the low point between Titterstone Clee and Clee Hill. This is *not* the Shropshire Way, which takes a more southeasterly direction. [West 1c]

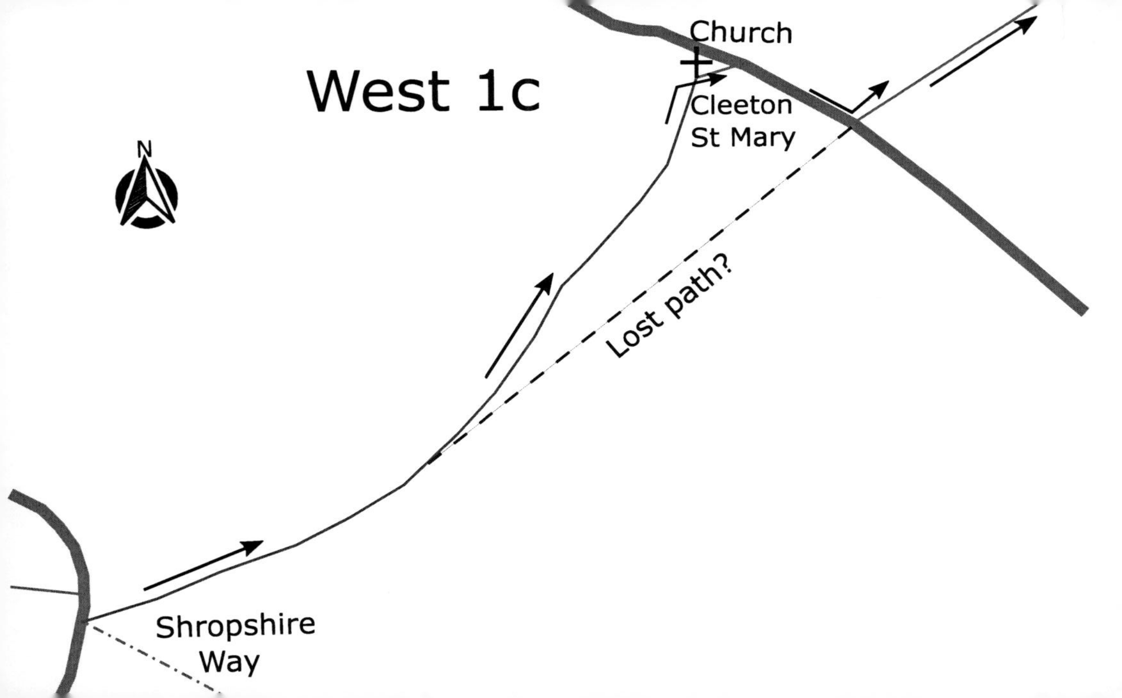
West 1c
N
Church
Cleeton
St Mary
Lost path?
Shropshire
Way

When you come to the corner of a field, you are close to another section of the original route which has been lost. The earliest OS map shows a road going northeast, but the walker now has to head on a more northerly line to come down to the village of Cleeton St Mary, the spire of its church being clearly visible from some distance.

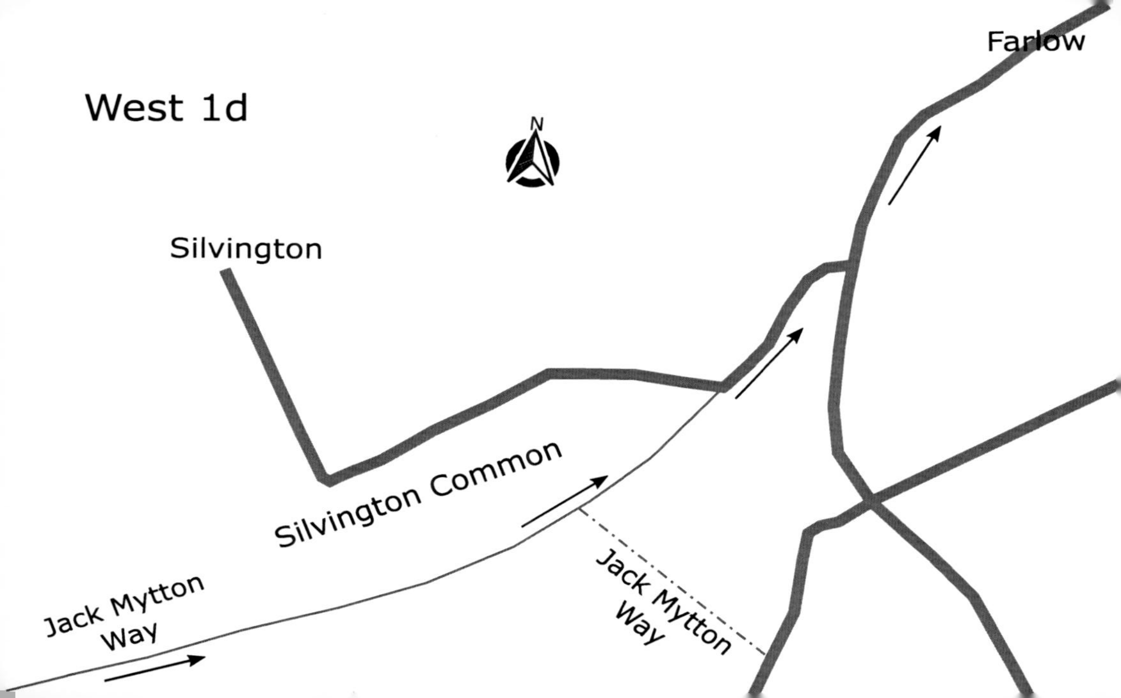
West 1d
N
Farlow
Silvington
Silvington Common
Jack Mytton Way
Jack Mytton Way

In the village, turn right and take the road to the east up to a farm (on your left) at a crossroads (where the lost section would have come). Turn left and you are back on the original route and can follow it on a ridgeway over Silvington Common, which can be purple with flowering heather in late summer, right down to Farlow, where the ridgeway ends. [See Map West 1d] It is about five miles from Bedlam to Farlow.

From Farlow, the old route is a narrow, tarmacked road with some deep holloways, via Well Farm, where you turn right for Prescott and then on to Bagginswood. It continues straight on (as a better road) through Bardley and down to join the B4363 briefly before turning right on the B4199 to reach Buttonbridge.

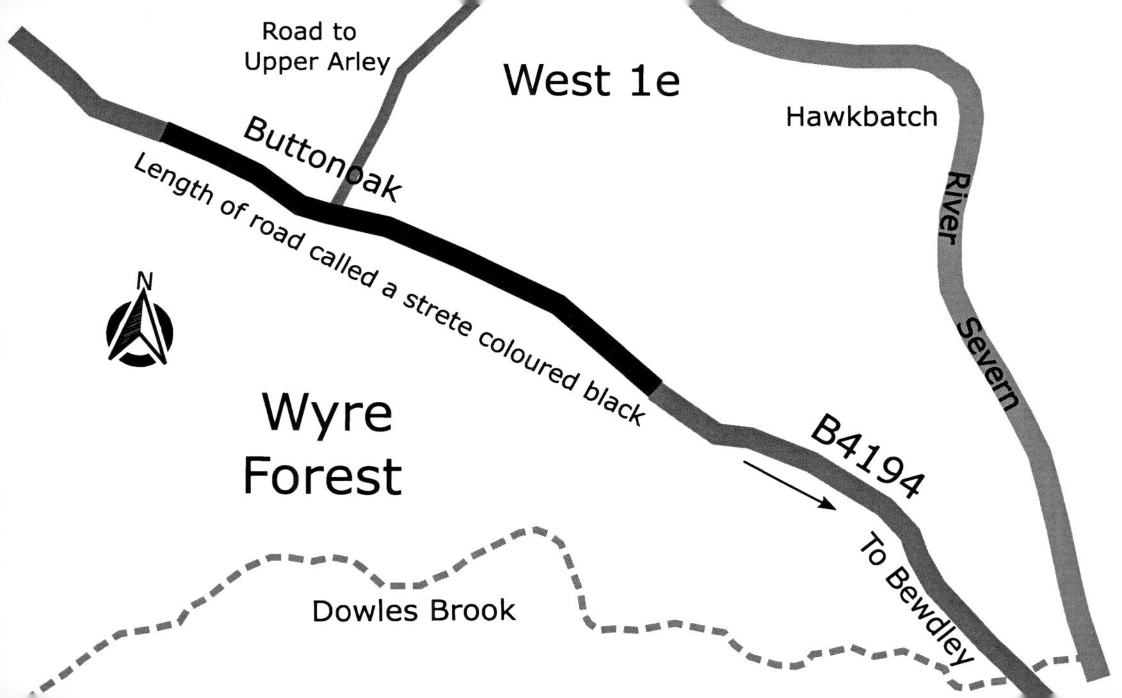
Road to
Upper Arley
West 1e
Hawkbatch
River Severn
Buttonoak
Length of road called a strete coloured black
N
Wyre
Forest
B4194
To Bewdley
Dowles Brook

The road from Buttonbridge is very straight, right down to Dowles and Bewdley and in an Anglo-Saxon charter of 996 for Upper Arley part of it is called a *strete*.[2] This suggests it had some kind of more durable surface, but it is not a Roman road – it is much earlier than that. The part that is the boundary mentioned in the charter is the section from SO747782 to SO765772 [shown black on Map West 1e].

---

[2] Della Hooke, *Worcestershire Anglo-Saxon Carter Bounds* (Studies in Anglo-Saxon History II, 1990), pp. 235-239

West 2 – Clows Top to Bewdley – 5½ miles

In 1935 G. B. Grundy set out the major prehistoric routes he believed passed through Worcestershire.[3] He suggested the Much Wenlock to Worcester ridgeway had a cross roads at Clows Top and that from that high point an ancient route went northeast to Bewdley. He called it Route 63. Coming from Clows Top on the A456, the main road passes the Colliers Arms and turns quite sharply left. There is a right-hand turning for Rock. This is at SO726724 and it is likely the ancient trackway continued straight on.

[See Map West 2a]

[3] G. B. Grundy, 'The ancient highways and tracks of Worcestershire and the middle Severn basin Pt.III', *Archaeological Journal*, Vol. 92 (1935), p. 118

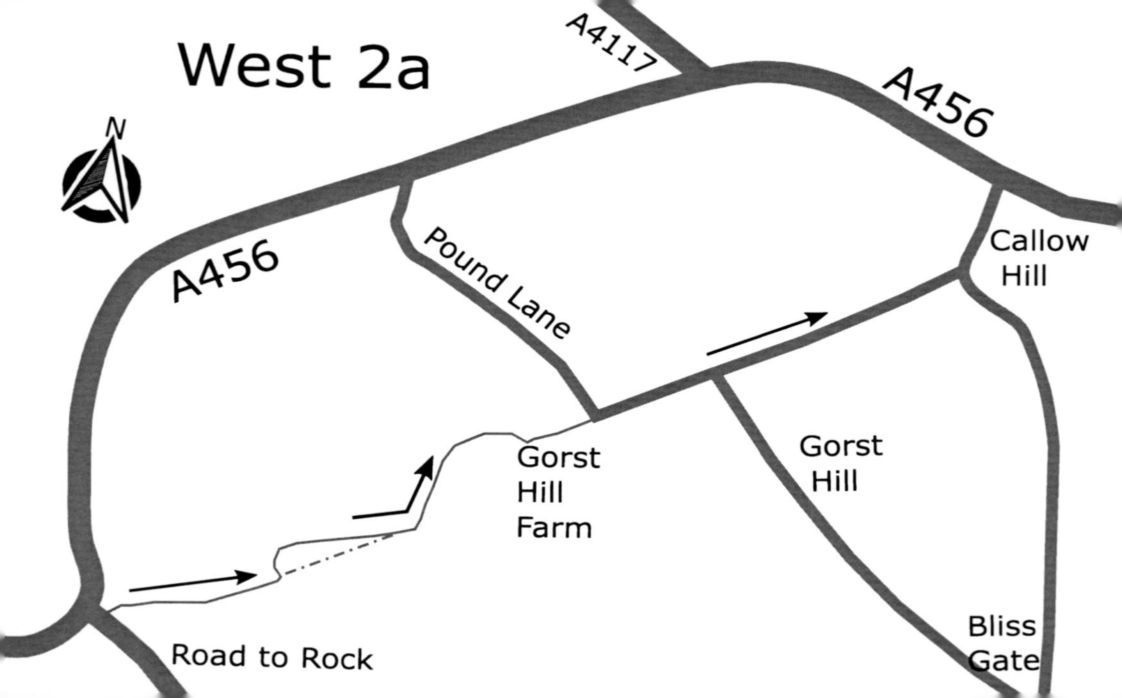
West 2a
N
A4117
A456
A456
Pound Lane
Callow Hill
Gorst Hill Farm
Gorst Hill
Road to Rock
Bliss Gate

To follow the old route take the Rock turning and very soon you will see a public bridleway indicated – it goes left up a tarmacked driveway which serves Oak View and The Homestead on your right, with another house on your left. This turns into a wide grassy path leading gently down to an opening between a fence and an old oak tree.

Continue through the opening and follow the pathway with the hedge on your left. Ahead of you across the field is Barrett's Cottage, a barn conversion. Barn Owls used to roost in these barns and may still use the hollow tree nearby.

As you round the corner, there is an old yew tree on your left. The original ancient route almost certainly went directly ahead and the OS map shows the footpath doing just that, but it is clear people walk around the left edge so as not to disturb the crop. So follow the hedgeline as it sweeps round this field. In the distance is Gorst Hill. As you come down to the bottom of the field, the trackway veers left through the trees; there may be a bridleway notice. The distance through the woodland is very short; you will see the gate at the bottom. Once through the gate, turn left up a very clear trackway. You soon cross a stream by an ancient oak tree.

There is a pathway straight up Gorst Hill which you will see signposted through a gate on the right, but this trackway you are on gives you a gentler climb. You pass between woodland on the left (where you may hear Goldcrests and Coal Tits singing from the conifers) and a hedge on the right and gradually climb up to Gorst Hill Farm, which is on your right. You then come gently down on a tarmacked drive to a gate (which you can walk round) onto the road. The ancient route would have gone straight ahead.

At this junction with Pound Lane continue straight on, going northeast. Give way at the road coming from Bliss Gate to join the main A456 at Callow Hill. The road from Cleobury Mortimer (the A4117) is clearly an old route. Grundy does not include it in his work and it does not follow a ridgeway. Perhaps it can be regarded as a secondary route.

You now turn right and follow the A456 down to Wharton Park, going past the Wyre Forest Visitor Centre and the Bewdley Business Park at Alton. This is Long Bank and it was once much wider. On the enclosure map for Rock[4] (made in 1820), there are small portions of land running along the roadside. These were taken into the adjoining properties, thus reducing the width of the road. Particularly wide roads of this nature are associated with droving, as the width meant there was plenty of room for the animals and also the grass verges supplied pasture to eat.

---

[4] Available on a CD at The Hive, Worcester

The droving of herds of animals from the place where they were reared to the place where they were sold for slaughter could be two thousand years old. Some old drovers' roads have been identified in the landscape, for instance, coming from Wales through the Midlands to go on to the markets in London. The drovers probably used existing trackways rather than creating totally fresh ones, but they would have made them wider than was necessary for a wagon so that there was pasture for the animals.

In our area, it is very likely that the road from Cleobury Mortimer, through Lem Hill, Pound Bank and on down the A456 to Bewdley was such a road. However, we believe the route existed before droving began. What we are trying to do is identify these really ancient routes.

Those used by pack horses tend to be narrower as the pack horses were strung out one behind the other. Pack horse bridges are also narrow, wide enough for a single horse, and with parapets low enough not to interfere with their packs. There probably were such bridges in our area in times past, but none seem to have survived to the present day.

Rosemary's photo of the donkey bridge over Borle Brook at SO726837

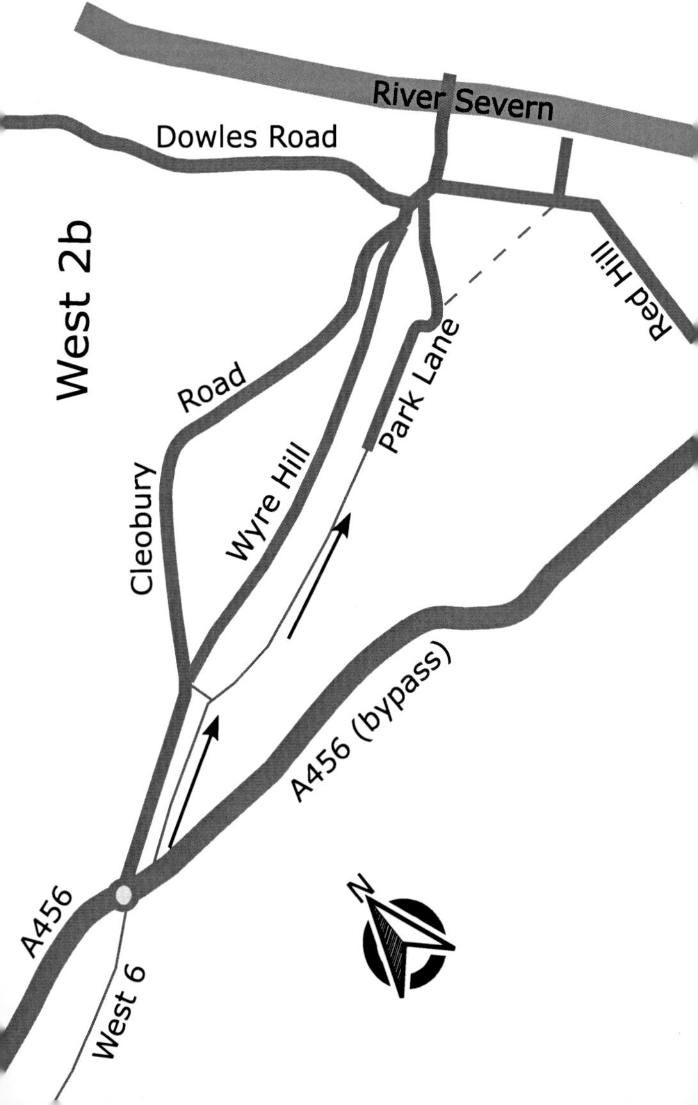
West 2b
River Severn
Dowles Road
Red Hill
Park Lane
Cleobury
Road
Wyre Hill
A456 (bypass)
A456
West 6
N

At the entrance to Wharton Park, [see Map West 2b] carefully cross the busy bypass and turn right to walk a short way down the verge to find some steps up on your left. These are not the best in the world so take care climbing up them. At the top, you go through a kissing gate and into a field. Follow the hedgeline left across the field past a beautiful tall old oak tree. Ahead of you is a wide gate, but when you get to it, you will find it is locked. There is, however, a short distance along the fence/hedge a stile over into the driveway you can see the other side.

Climb over the stile and turn right to follow the driveway round almost into a residential conversion of some farm buildings. Over on your right, you will see a wide kissing gate giving access to a track through a yard. Follow the track and then bear left, going slightly downhill. Along the other side of a fence you will see a pathway which goes through a kissing gate and into a green area. The ancient route almost certainly came through here, but has been badly disrupted by buildings and industry.

You have left behind the cars and the hard surfaces, but now face what can be a muddy pathway through the field. You are walking parallel to Wyre Hill and soon come to a house blocking the direct route, so you turn right. There is a path going left which would take you out onto Wyre Hill by Summerdyne Nursing Home. Having turned right, you soon turn left again in order to maintain the direct route into Bewdley. There are houses on your left and a fence on your right, but the trackway is wide and there are many old oak trees in the left-hand boundary.

You walk past the back of St Anne's School. Notice how wide this trackway is. At the end of the school property, you need to ignore the paths going right and left and instead go through the kissing gate and into what is Park Lane. You pass four houses on your right before coming out onto the tarmacked road.

The ancient route continues down Park Lane as far as Barretts Style, which goes off to the left. This was the major access way into Bewdley in the past. Wyre Hill runs parallel to Park Lane, but is thought to be a development made in the 1460s, with plots being laid out either side, those on the southeast linking through to Park Lane. The Cleobury Road is even more recent, being created in the late eighteenth century as a turnpike road.

It is not easy to trace the course of the ancient route through Bewdley itself. It probably came down the narrow part of Park Lane to the junction with Snuff Mill Walk and then went straight on over Tickenhill, heading for the ford at the bottom of Lax Lane. It is unlikely that Load Street was part of it because the river at the end of Load Street is deep, whereas the river at the end of Lax Lane is much shallower. (See 2009 photo below)

To walk this last part, we suggest you turn right onto Hernes Nest (opposite Barretts Stile) and after a short distance you will find a footpath going downhill on your left. This will bring you out onto Snuff Mill Walk and avoids the very narrow part of Park Lane (somewhat hazardous for pedestrians). Where Snuff Mill Walk meets Park Lane, on your right you will see the entrance to Tickenhill. Go up there and on your right you will find a gate leading into a footpath which takes you round the side of the hill and gives you lovely views across to Kateshill House and St Anne's House. At the other end, take the path to your right and go straight down, over a pathway and into a narrow path along the backs of the houses. You pass a timber framed building on the gable end of which is the date of 1607; actually, the house was built in 1599 as a grammar school and the date may have something to do with James I granting a fresh charter a bit later. At the bottom, you pass the former Oddfellows Convalescent Home and turn left to go down Park Alley and out onto High Street. To reach the Lax shoal, you need to cross over the road, turn right past the Pack Horse Public House and then turn left down Lax Lane. All these buildings have interrupted the ancient route.

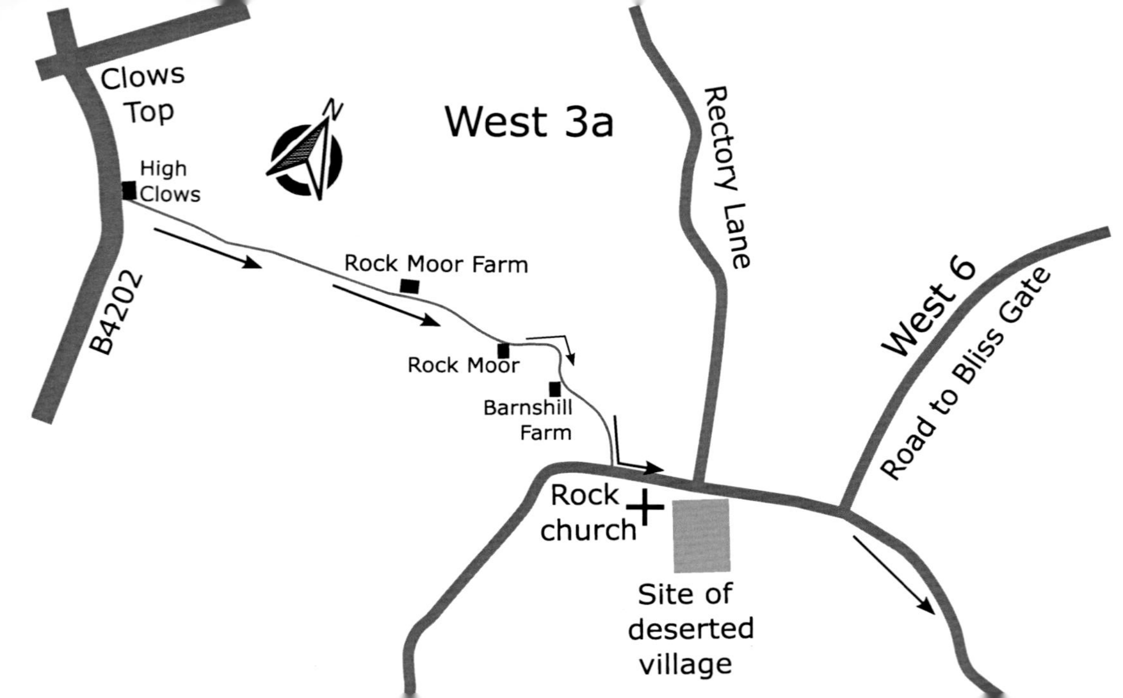

Clows Top
West 3a
High Clows
B4202
Rock Moor Farm
Rock Moor
Barnshill Farm
Rectory Lane
West 6
Road to Bliss Gate
Rock church
Site of deserted village

West 3 – High Clows to Dunley – 5½ miles

Grundy believed there was another route going east from Clows Top and he called this Route 64. It began a short distance along the B4202 at High Clows and headed for Rock. The footpath can be found on the south side of the buildings which make up High Clows. [See Map West 3a] A faded footpath sign on the fence points you to follow the fence into a yard with a wooden barn on your right. Ahead is a gate with a wobbly stile to its right. Climb over and head for the far right-hand corner of the field.

There is some evidence that the trackway would have followed the right-hand hedgeline (this is the line shown on the OS map) and near the bottom you can see how steep the side of the ditch is, but it is impossible to walk it. There is now a wide entrance into another field where footpaths converge. The original route almost certainly goes straight ahead (where you can see an old caravan in the undergrowth), but it cannot be walked until it turns into a wide trackway further on. To reach the wide trackway, you have to go round. The easiest (but illegal!) way is to go right through an open gate and keep fairly close to the hedgeline on your left. At the end of the field, you will find a stile on your left and crossing that brings you into the wide trackway opposite a magnificent oak. A more difficult (but official) route is to bear left through a gap in the fence, across the tussocks and then part way through the field, bear right to get down to a stile in the far corner. That stile takes you into the wide trackway. Walk east along this wonderful greenway. Over to your right you can see Rock Church tower. The church is early 12th century and the tower dates from 1510; so travellers have been able to use the tower as a guiding point in the landscape for more than five hundred years.

You pass a lake on your left and the buildings of Rock Moor Farm, before going through a wide gate. The track turns from grass to a harder surface, as this is the driveway for several buildings. Follow this driveway as it winds its way and becomes tarmacked near Rock Moor, where there is a huge walnut tree on the right.

Further on you pass the entrance to Barnshill Farm (there is no notice to say this) on your right with a clear 'No vehicular access' sign, unless the gate is open. There is a footpath the other side of the hedge, but stay on the lane (the tarmac is somewhat rough in places) to come out onto the road. Turn left and you will soon find yourself walking past the church at Rock.

On the eastern side of the church is evidence of a deserted village. [See Map] There is a footpath through the hedge opposite Rectory Lane which traverses the field and gives a view of the earthworks.

Map of deserted village

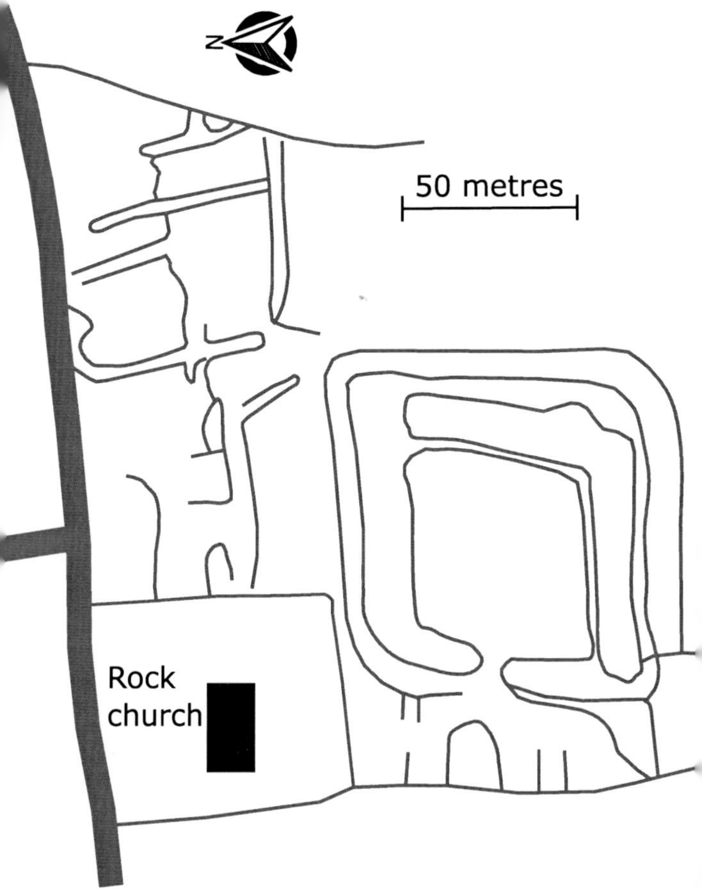

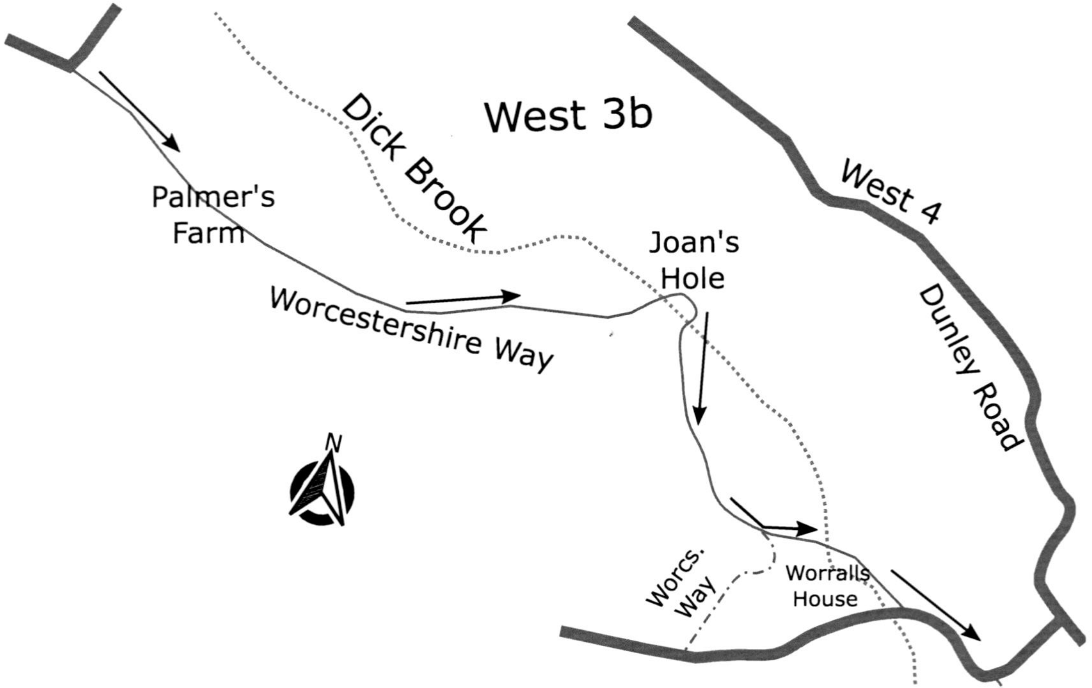
West 3b
Dick Brook
West 4
Dunley Road
Palmer's Farm
Worcestershire Way
Joan's Hole
Worcs. Way
Worralls House
N

From Rock church keep to the main road along the Greenway past Goddess Farm and Castle Farm. Where the road goes sharply left and downhill (where the banks are full of wild flowers in springtime), turn right along a trackway towards Palmers Farm. [Move on to Map West 3b] This is the Worcestershire Way (indicated with the picture of a pear) and a very clear ridgeway, with good views either side. Skylarks sing high in the air above arable fields. To the left Heightington is clearly visible (unless you are in thick mist!); that is another ridgeway route (see Walk West 4).

Grundy goes no further than Joan's Hole in his description. This is where the ridgeway ends and the ancient path becomes unclear. There is a modern footpath which crosses Dick Brook, goes past a house called Joan's Hole and then crosses back over the Brook. The 1842 Tithe Map for Rock[5] clearly shows that the trackway went into the Brook for more than a hundred yards before returning to dry land – no problem if you are riding a horse! The bridle path even today goes through this section of the Brook.

A Kingfisher may be spotted if you are lucky and Grey Wagtails may be seen bobbing along the water's edge.

---

[5] Available on a CD at The Hive, Worcester

Once clear of the Brook, there is a holloway up through the trees and a gate into a field. Part way along the path, leave the Worcestershire Way at a marker post (half way across the second field), veer off to the left and head for a path through the trees and into the private garden of Worrall's House; this is still a public footpath. You cross a bridge to exit the garden and then head across the field (the former mill is on your right) to the road. Turn left to walk up and round to a sharp left-hand turn which takes you to the junction with the road coming down from Heightington, Grundy's Route 67 (see Walk West 4).

The ancient trackway is unlikely to have done this sharp left-hand turn and in fact there is a footpath straight ahead, to the left of a property called The Driftway.

(Driftway is another word for a drovers' road, so maybe cattle were driven along here or the owners simply chose an interesting name.) It brings you down to a farmer's track, where you need to turn right; originally the route was probably direct from the tarmacked road, but has been compromised by the dwelling and its garden. The track you are now on goes west to Netherton House, but there is a left turn which follows the contours to the main road and could eventually have led the traveller to a crossing of the Severn at Astley (there were shoals at both Hampstall SO813676 and at Wyre SO814657). The alternative is to turn left and go east along the farmer's track and you will come to Dunley, where the most direct way to the Severn is to head for Astley Cross, Hermitage Way and Redstone.

West 4a

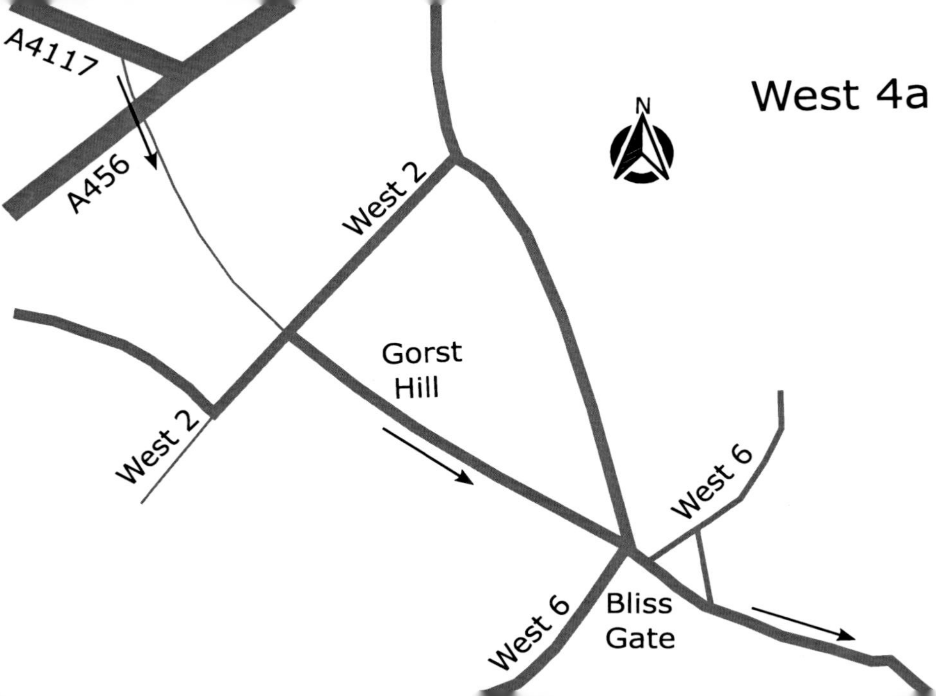

West 4 – Far Forest to Dunley – 5 miles

Grundy has another pre-historic route which goes through Bliss Gate. This could be linked to his Route 63 at about SO738732, where a lane from Bliss Gate turns into a footpath as it goes northwest. He called it Route 67. [Map West 4a]

We will begin on the Far Forest road, the A4117, not far from its junction with the A456, at the notice which says 'Give Way 185 yards'. Go through the gate. Continue for a short distance and then the path opens out. The original trackway probably went straight ahead (through a slight holloway), but it is now overgrown and impassable, so the path bears left. There is a house on your left and in front a meadow full of wild flowers in the summer, but there is usually a path cut for walkers.

The grasslands in the Wyre area originate from forest clearance and land taken from the former commons and wood pastures. They often have poor acid soils and have not been intensively farmed, which means wild flowers can flourish. The grass is best not cut until August or September and is then left to dry before being removed. If cut as early as July, the edge can be left uncut as a refuge for grasshoppers because their nymphs are most vulnerable then.

Walk through to the far side and be very careful how you exit the field as there is a dilapidated gate and a wire across the path. This is the A456 and is very busy, so cross with care and then go through the small gate on the other side. There is a wide track with conifers on your left and a field on your right which used to be an orchard and now is part of a private garden. You may glimpse some old fruit trees through the conifers to the left; beyond that field is the Far Forest Sports Centre.

The wide track narrows to a path through trees with a wire fence on the left. Great Spotted Woodpeckers, Nuthatches and Treecreepers are present in the woodland and Bluebells flower here in the spring. At the end of the woodland is a wooden bridge over a stream (actually Gladder Brook). The next section can be very muddy, but is short and leads into an open field where you turn left and follow a faint track which will take you round to the right, through some scrub (and mud!) to another bridge over a stream. You emerge onto a cultivated field. If the path is not obvious, you need to walk straight ahead;

you will see a building on the brow of the hill – head for the tree to the right of that.

At the top, there is a break in the fence and the footpath is indicated as going slightly to the right. There are two drives here; the one to the right serves Alton Cross Cottage and the other to the left The Cottage. If you walk down the Alton Cross

Cottage drive, you will find a 'Private' sign the other end! It is not clear which drive should be used by walkers. When you reach the road, the footpath sign suggests you should use The Cottage drive and an old map does the same. Cross the road (you have crossed Walk West 2 at this point) and continue on the tarmacked road to Bliss Gate. You are now on a very clear ancient route right through to Dunley.

Bliss Gate appears to get its name from some kind of toll gate. When the Mortimer family divided their manor of Bewdley and 'sublet' the Ribbesford part (in the mid 12th century), they retained the finger of land which ran southwest. [See Map of the division of the manor] The road at Bliss Gate passes through this piece of their territory and looks very much like an expression of their control of its traffic.

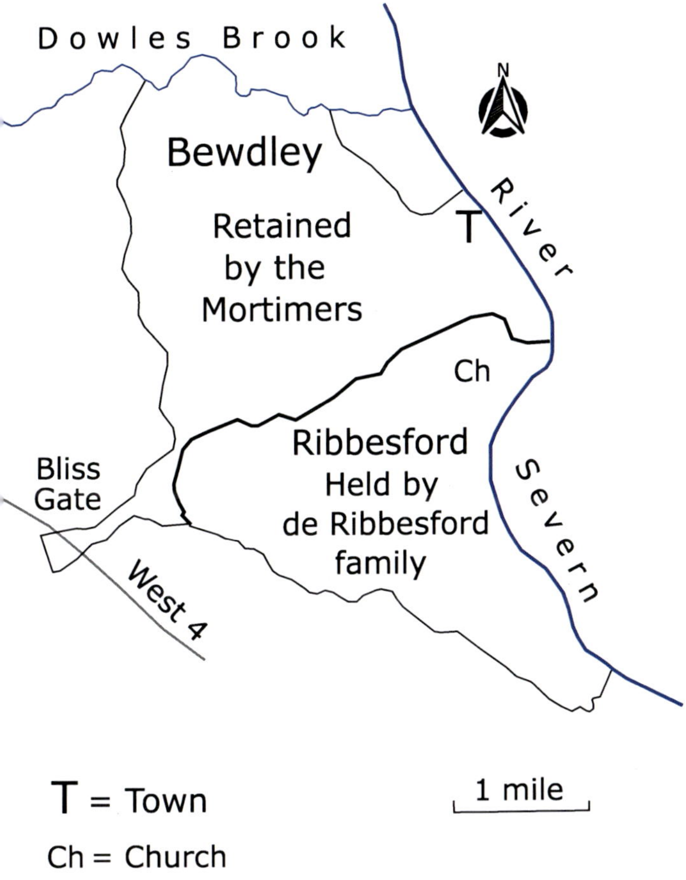

Division of the Manor

The route goes down the lane southeast to Heightington. You will pass St Giles' church, a small rectangular stone building of the early 13th century. The bell turret is probably 17th century and the porch is 18th century. The church is not usually locked, so do go inside. The walls are plastered, but early wall paintings have been discovered below the current surface. In the north wall, near the east end, is an early 13th century lancet window; the other windows are later. [Move on to Map West 4b]

This is another clear ridgeway and you can look across to the right (see photo) to see the ridgeway referred in Walk West 3. These two routes may have been in use at the same time, but in view of the difficulties presented by the topography at Joan's Hole, it seems likely that the Heightington road became the preferred trackway.

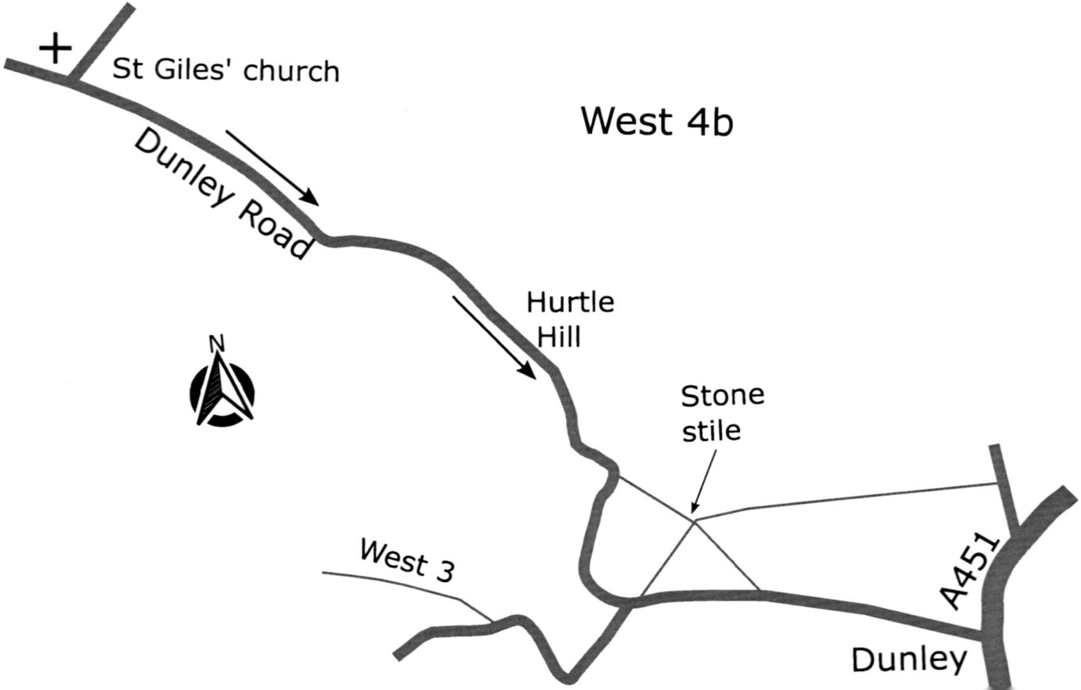
St Giles' church
West 4b
Dunley Road
Hurtle
Hill
N
Stone
stile
West 3
A451
Dunley

At the end of the ridgeway, where the road bears right, there is a footpath on the left which continues the line of the road.

The footpath notice is hidden in the hedge, but points into the driveway of Hurtle Top. Keep the garage and house on your right and bear slightly right, down to the bottom of the driveway and you will find a small gap in the hedge. You emerge onto a trackway. Stop and admire the view. To your left is Stourport and beyond are the Clent Hills. To your right is Abberley and in the far distance Malvern. Envy the people who live with this view! The path goes over the track and straight down the hill, at the bottom of which is a collapsed stone stile, a very unusual feature. (See photo on the next page)

There are two paths. One goes straight ahead of you and comes out onto the road.

The other bears slightly left and heads for Burnthorne Farm. This might have been the original line of the route down to a crossing of the Severn at Redstone.

At the bottom of the ridgeway, the tarmacked road continues on to Dunley where you meet the A451, but it seems unlikely this is an ancient route as the way is cut through the rock at one point and that must be a more recent feature, although it is possible that the old trackway went over the top of the rocky outcrop and the cutting was made later but on the same line. Routes will have changed once wheeled vehicles were using them.

At the main road, go right for a short distance and then turn left on to a lane. After about half a mile, you cross the B4194 and then over another cross roads at Astley Cross. Keep going straight on until the road peters out at a caravan site. Beyond this point are the Redstone caves and the site of the Redstone Ford, a well-known medieval crossing point of the Severn. The River Severn is also a wildlife corridor; in recent years there has been an increase in animals such as Otters, Goosanders and Kingfishers, indicating that there are still plenty of fish in the river.

It is said[6] that until the building of the bridge at Stourport in 1775, the main place to cross the Severn in that area was at Redstone, where there was a ford and, later, a ferry. The river here has been altered so much that it is hard to imagine any traffic over the river at this point. However, assuming this statement is correct means that coaches as well as pedestrians and horse riders were using these ridgeway routes to move through the landscape. As already mentioned, it seems the Heightington route would have been easier and perhaps that is why it became a tarmacked road and the other ridgeway track is only a path in places.

---

[6] E.g. John Noake, *Guide to Worcestershire* (London, 1868), p. 21

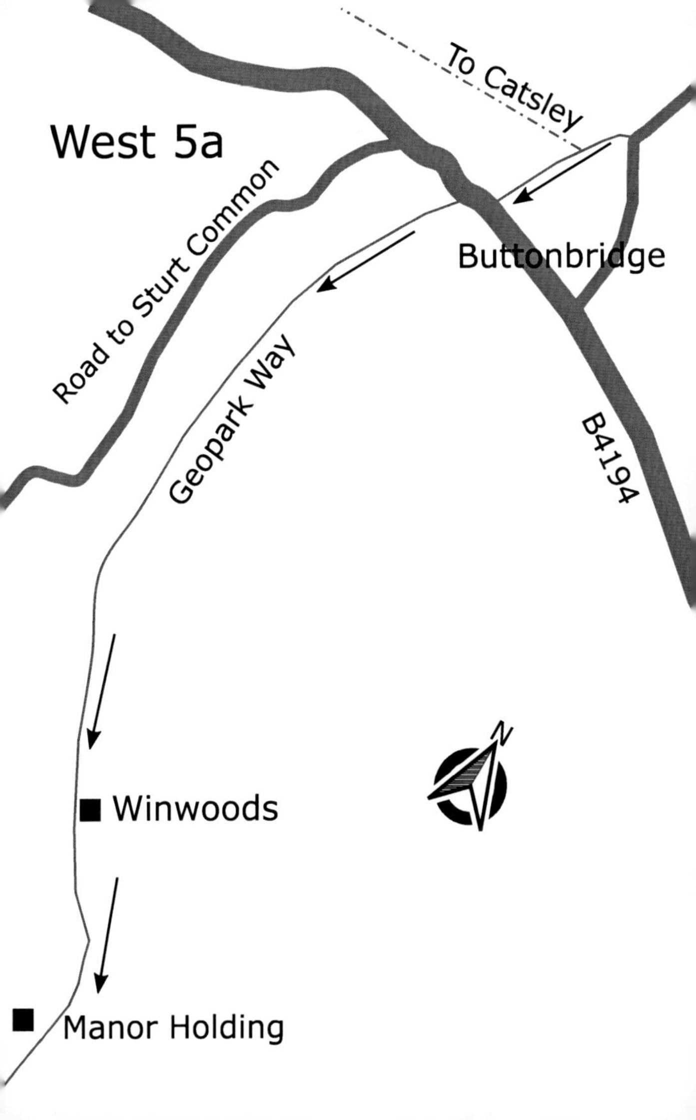
West 5a
To Catsley
Road to Sturt Common
Buttonbridge
Geopark Way
B4194
N
Winwoods
Manor Holding

West 5 – Buttonbridge to Dowles Brook – 2½ miles

There is a major ridgeway running through Chelmarsh in Shropshire. Indeed the ridgeway route can be traced almost from Bridgnorth as far south as Highley. To the southwest of Highley the route becomes obscure, but there must have been a way over the Borle Brook. South of the Brook, there is a path from Tip House to Coppice Gate where you can walk on a tarmacked lane for about a quarter of a mile. Where the lane bears left, there is an entrance to a number of holdings including Dormer Cottage at SO733796. On the left of the entrance, you will find a stile giving access to a footpath. [See Map West 5a]

The stile is marked with the logo for the Geopark Way, which is a 109 mile walking trail through the Abberley and Malvern Hills Geopark. It was the brainchild of the Herefordshire and Worcestershire Earth Heritage Trust and the route was published in 2009. It is designed to illustrate 'the 700 million years old history of this part of the Earth's crust, which has resulted in some of the best rural scenery that England has to offer'. This walk is only about two miles, but you could follow the Geopark Way right down to Bewdley if you wish. The logo is a stylised image of the trilobite *Dalmanites*.

This stile can be skirted, but many of the stiles on this route are not easy and some are in a bad condition. You have been warned! The path hugs a hedge of mainly holly on the right. You will see a footpath (with a stile) going off to the right; this goes to Catsley Farm, but you go straight on to the next stile. Again, keep to the hedge and you will soon come to a stile at the main road, the B4194, at Buttonbridge. After climbing this, turn right and walk along the verge for about 50m. Then take care crossing the road directly in line with the electricity pylon to pick up the footpath on the opposite side. The stile is marked Geopark Way.

The road you have just crossed is the Clun-Clee ridgeway, named by Lily Chitty and described in Walk West 1. So this point at Buttonbridge may be the meeting place of two major ridgeway routes, one coming from the north and one coming from the west. The Clun-Clee route continues down to the Severn at Bewdley, but the path going almost due south from Buttonbridge eventually links with the Worcestershire routes suggested by Grundy as being prehistoric.

Once over the stile, you find yourself in a private garden with a boating lake. You need to keep close to the bushes on your right and will see ahead of you a stile over the fence, next to one of the tall poplar trees. This stile is very difficult; it takes you into a cultivated field. If the field is newly ploughed or newly sown, then you will have to forge a path directly across. You will see a line of poplars in the distance; you are heading for the right-hand end of that line, where you will find yet another stile in the hedgerow.

From this field, you get views to the north of the Clee hills.

On the other side of the hedge, come through the tiny copse and bear slightly left to find the next stile into a field of sheep. Keep to the left-hand side in the first field and then go diagonally across the next field. There is a marker post and in the right-hand corner is another stile. Beyond that is another area of grass (which sometimes has sheep) and a short walk straight ahead to the next stile. Now you walk over some grass to cross an access road leading to a development of chalets. The path continues through a gate in the hedge with a clear Geopark Way marker.

Keep to the left through this large field, where a lone oak tree stands proud. Again over to your right are views of Titterstone Clee and further to the right is Brown Clee. The hedge appears, in some places at least, to mask a holloway, but it is too overgrown to be walked.

At the end of the hedge is a trackway. Go straight ahead up the trackway and follow this. To your right (behind the hedge) the land is fairly flat, but to your left the land is open and falls away quite sharply. Travellers would have had a good view of their surroundings.

Walk on this track south and you will come to Winwoods; bear right at the big barn and you will find a very convenient bench on which to take a rest. Several fields near here are flower-rich and margins along arable fields have been planted up with seed harvested locally to provide nectar for butterflies and other invertebrates.

Walk on south, ignoring the farm's driveway going off to the right; keep on the lane with grass up the centre. Just south of the farm, the track divides, the left-hand track swinging away to the left. There is another footpath here and this is also the rough location where you cross the Elan Valley water pipeline, though there is no evidence above ground of its presence at this point. There is a marker post in the hedge saying there is a footpath to the left (Walk West 10) and one straight ahead which is the Geopark Way. You need to go straight ahead and over a stile. You then walk through this grassy field, keeping the hedge on your right. You will come to a kissing gate, leading into another field. Ahead of you the house known as Kingswood is visible. In some fields, you will see many mole hills; these are more likely to occur where the ground has not been the subject of artificial fertiliser and pesticides. Again, keep to the right and you come to yet another kissing gate; this one gives access to a narrow pathway which brings you on to a drive.

On your right you will see a timber framed building; this is known as Manor Holding. The building is 17th century, with a 19th century extension. [Move on to Map West 5b]

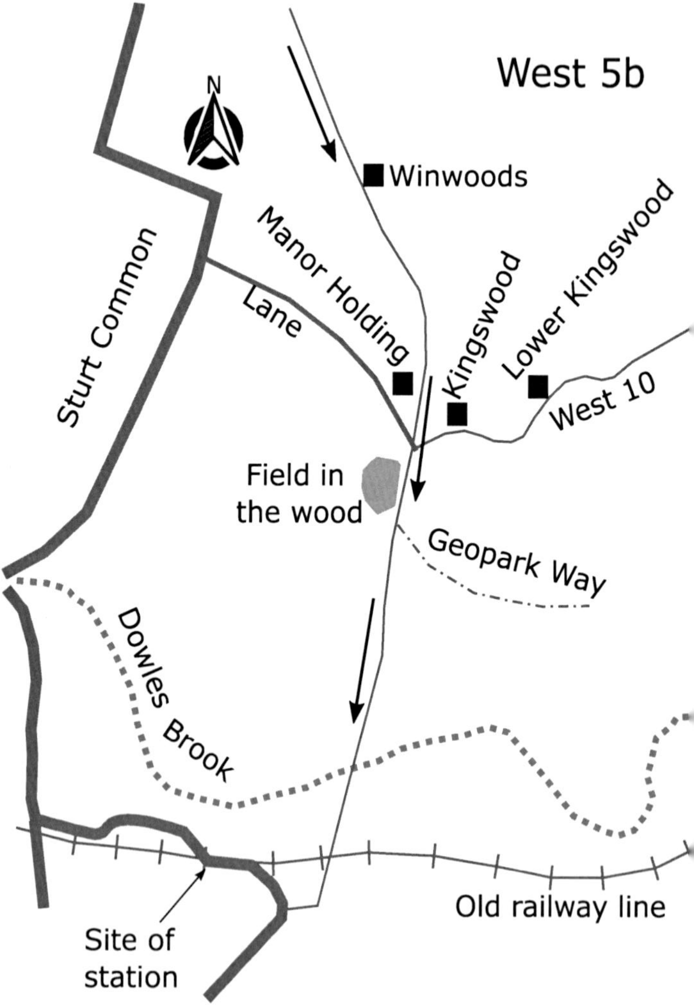

N
West 5b
Winwoods
Manor Holding
Lane
Sturt Common
Kingswood
Lower Kingswood
West 10
Field in the wood
Geopark Way
Dowles Brook
Old railway line
Site of station

Keeping the buildings on your right, walk down the drive until it meets a lane which leads to Kingswood and Lower Kingswood.

This is a very interesting area. There is evidence of an Iron Age settlement at Kingswood, within the private grounds of Lower Kingswood. The place takes its name from belonging, it is thought, to Henry I. The name suggests that the Wyre Forest was probably not in royal hands, otherwise there would be no point in singling out what was the King's wood. There is a reference in 1296 to a deer park at Kingswood. John de Seagrave complained about those who 'broke his park and entered his chase at Kyngeswode, county Salop, hunted therein and carried away deer.' This would be a bigger area than the possible Iron Age enclosure surrounding Lower Kingswood, but could have included it.

The distance from the stile at Dormer Cottage to the Kingswood lane is just under two miles.

At the point where the drive meets the lane, you need to bear slightly to the left; you will see a barrier and beside it a marked path, which you follow next.

Here the walker plunges into the woodland of the Wyre Forest. On the right, however, is a cleared area, known as the 'Field in the Wood' and full of mounds which are the nests of Yellow Meadow Ants. A LiDAR image shows what looks like ridge and furrow in this field, which is somewhat unusual for this area, but some of the other fields also show faint evidence of ridge and furrow cultivation. There could be a clearing of the land at Kingswood because the soil was suitable for growing grass or crops, so Winwoods and Kingswood could well have been free of forest trees for hundreds of years. It is very interesting to overlay a map of the geology of this area; it immediately becomes apparent that the pasture land is above different rocks from the land given over to trees. [See Geology map] In simple geological terms Greater Wyre is a mixture of Etruria Mudstone and Siltstone with some areas of Halesowen Sandstone. (See *The Nature of Wyre* pp. 18-19) Note how most of the woodland is on the Mudstone/Siltstone, while the Halesowen Sandstone clearly provides more productive soils for agriculture.

The path goes almost due south to the Dowles Brook. You will pass a footpath for the Geopark Way on your left, but ignore that. When you get to the Brook, you face a challenge. The footbridge here is unsafe and cannot be used. It is sometimes possible to get across the Brook using stepping stones when the water level is low. You might like to pause to admire the variety of ferns, mosses and liverworts growing along the banks of the stream in this cool and shaded valley.

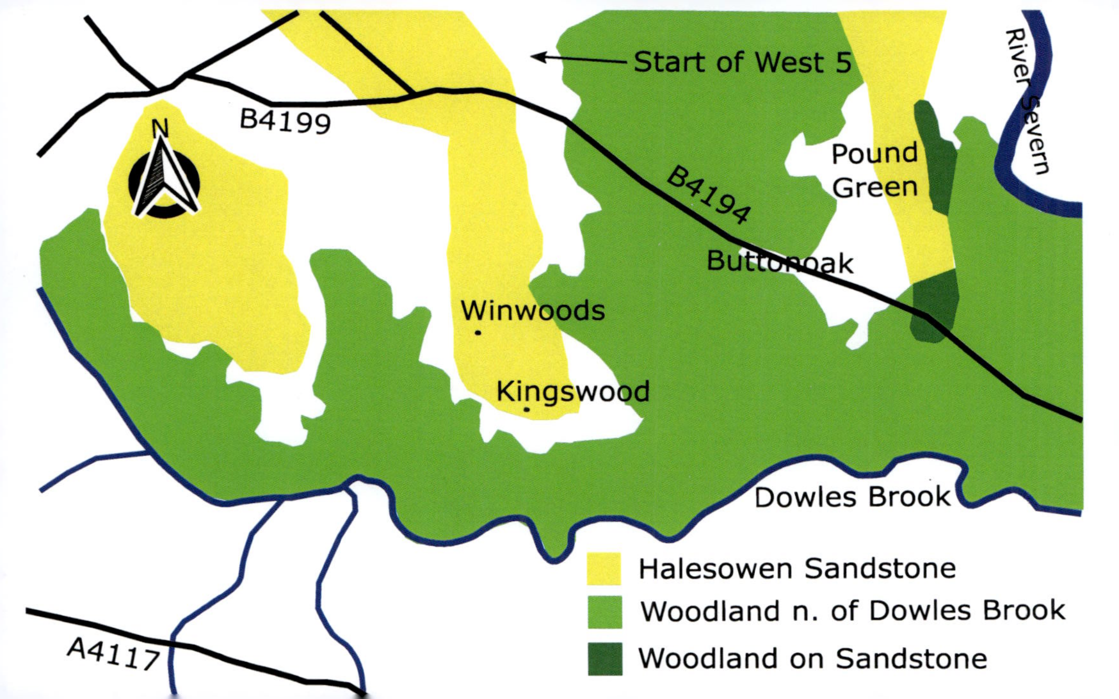
River Severn
Start of West 5
Pound
Green
B4199
B4194
Buttonoak
Winwoods
Kingswood
Dowles Brook
A4117
N
Halesowen Sandstone
Woodland n. of Dowles Brook
Woodland on Sandstone

If you manage to get across without getting too wet, then you will find a path rising up, past a cottage on your right. It comes to the site of the old railway line which crossed over the road by means of a bridge. This bridge has been dismantled so you now walk through a cutting. You will come up the track to find a house on your left; this is called Newalls and was once owned by Norman Hickin, famous for his books about the Wyre Forest. The road turns right and continues as a holloway.

The ancient trackway from here on is unclear. Perhaps you might like to work out where you think it went! It needs to link up with perhaps Walk West 4 or the Much Wenlock ridgeway which goes through Clows Top.

Walk at Far Forest

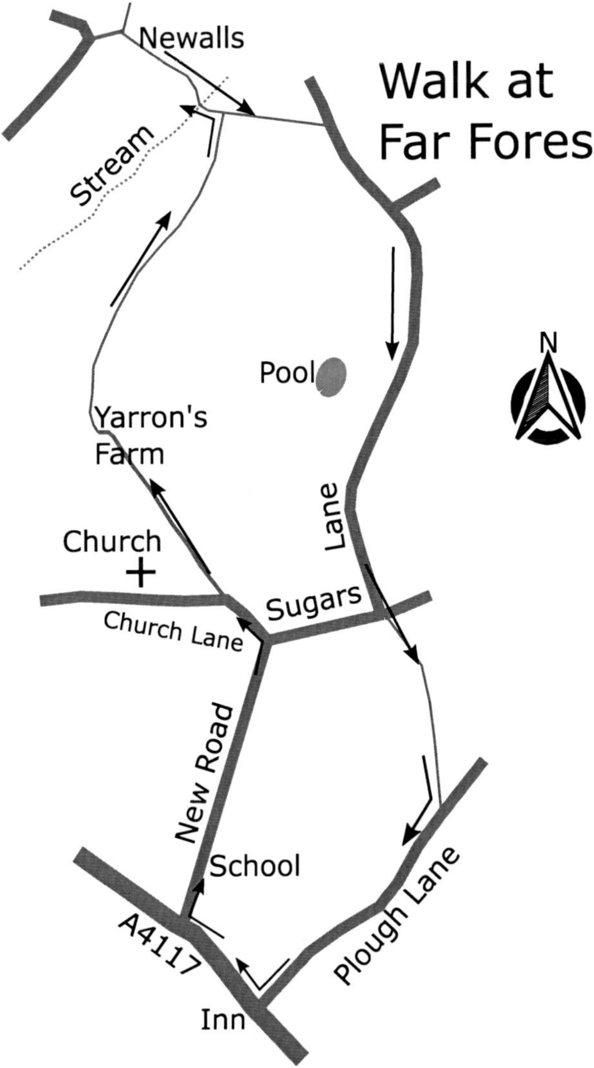

A walk at Far Forest – 2¼ miles

As the ancient route is unknown, here is a pleasant circular walk with some interesting features. Starting at the point near Newalls where the lane makes a right-angled bend (SO728758), take the footpath which goes left through a gate; it is marked ‘Cleobury Country Walk’ with the image of the church spire. After a short distance you are in a holloway which takes you down to a stream, which is crossed by a bridge. (See photo on the next page) Bear left up the hill. At the top, you will see a stile on your right; ignore this for now – you will cross it at the end of the walk. Continue down the holloway to another stream; this one is crossed by walking over a large drainage pipe. The path then goes straight up the hill and is not difficult to follow.

At the top, bear right and you come out onto a tarmacked road near a house called Forest Dell.

Turn right to walk along the road or use the grassy verge. You pass a notice which tells you it is a private road leading to 'Far Forest Caravan Park'. This is a surprisingly wide road and was perhaps an old trackway. It can also be very busy, so look out for traffic! Join Sugars Lane which comes in from the left and continue along the road. You will pass on your right a property (Sugars Farm on some maps) which overlooks a large lake and, later, on your left the entrance to the Hillview Caravan Park. Where the road suddenly turns sharp right, there is a footpath straight ahead, to the right of a driveway to a farm. To the left is Lynalls Lane. There is a stile which can be walked round. The path follows the edge of an open field, with a hedge on your left. At the end is a kissing gate which takes you into a narrow path for a short distance before you pass through another gate to come out on to Plough Lane by a property called Cleestones. Turn right and follow Plough Lane to the main road, the A4117. The Plough Inn is opposite.

If you want to continue on an ancient route, you can turn left and walk up the footpath alongside the road until you see the sign on the other side which says 'Give Way 185 yards'. You can now pick up Walk West 4.

To continue the circular route around Far Forest, turn right to walk along the footpath beside the main road. You pass the village shop and the Baptist Church. Turn right down New Road, walk on past the Lea Memorial School (built in 1903) and some houses to the junction with Sugars Lane (this is the road you were on earlier) and turn left down Church Lane. After a short distance, take the right-hand lane marked with a dead end sign. Over to the left you will see Far Forest Church. This was built in 1846 and a parish was carved out for it from Bewdley, Ribbesford and Stottesdon. On the right, you pass the Far Forest Centre, which has in the past been used by groups of young people; the site faces redevelopment. The lane soon ceases to be tarmacked and becomes a rough track.

This lane leads to Yarron's Farm and the path goes through the middle of it. After you pass the house on your left, the track bears right. A footpath goes off to the left, but stick with the main trackway through the farmyard and go down the hill, past a newly built barn. Part way down the hill, the footpath crosses to the other side of the hedgeline, so you need to go through a gate on your left in order to walk on down the hill with the trees on your right. Where the ground falls away more steeply and you see a wooded area on your right, you need to bear slightly left to find the stile in the middle of the boundary at the bottom of the field. Cross this stile and, if necessary, fight your way through the brambles for a short distance before you come to another stile, which you should recognise as you passed this near the beginning of the walk. You turn left to retrace your steps back to the starting point.

Animal tracks

In soft mud or snow, tracks can often by seen. On the next two pages are some examples. In the first picture, the rabbit was hopping along in the direction of the human, putting its 2 front paws down first (shown at the back) followed by the back feet (shown in front) which come forward and to the side of the forefeet.

3 mammals have walked here - human, Fallow Deer and the small Reeves Muntjac deer

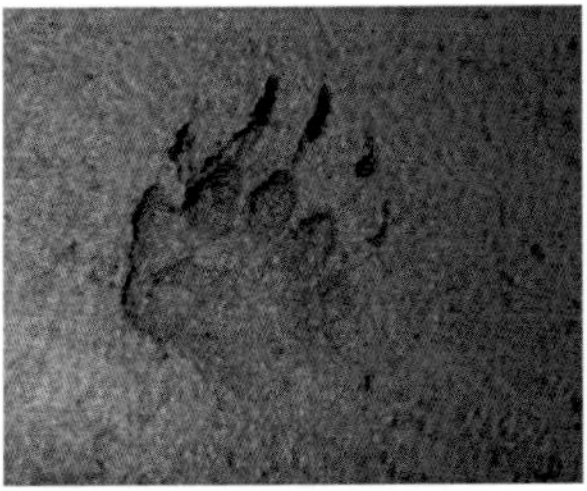

A Badger front foot print in soft mud shows pads in a line and long claw marks

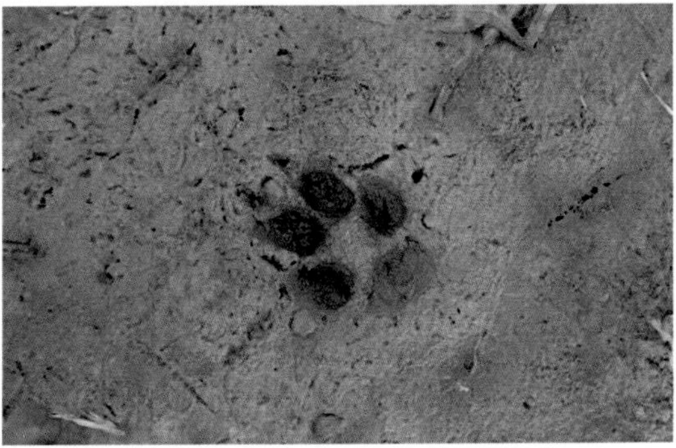

This Fox has left its symmetrical print with, unlike most dogs, a gap between the front and back pads

West 6 – Rock to Wharton Park – 3 miles

The National Archives at Kew hold a map dated to 1515 of part of Bewdley Park.[7] The area is crossed by a path described as: "Heretofore the way from Linedon to Beawdley being a wayne way but now a way only for empty waynes and horses". (Wayne/wain is a wagon.) This has been identified as lying between Lye Head and Long Bank and is still a footpath. As we know it was a way for carts long before 1515, we can assume this is an old route between Rock (Lindon) and Bewdley.

Beginning near Rock Church at SO735712 (on Walk West 3), there is a lane that goes north by the Rock Cross Inn called Quarry Road. Incidentally, there is also a footpath which goes south past

[7] TNA ref: MPB/17

Bowercourt Farm and Lower Snead Farm to come out on the Much Wenlock to Worcester ridgeway at Abberley (SO744682) near the entrance to Beehive Farm. However, we are going north to Bewdley.

Go up Quarry Road northeast past Bullockhurst Farm, down a steep hill into the valley and over the brook. As you climb up the other side you find yourself in a wonderful holloway suggesting this is an ancient route. Further on there is another section where the road is deep set between banks. When you come to Bliss Gate, there are three roads. The road to the left goes through Gorst Hill and the ancient traveller could have then pursued a route through to Far Forest and even to Buttonbridge and Bridgnorth (see Walks West 4 and 5).

West 6

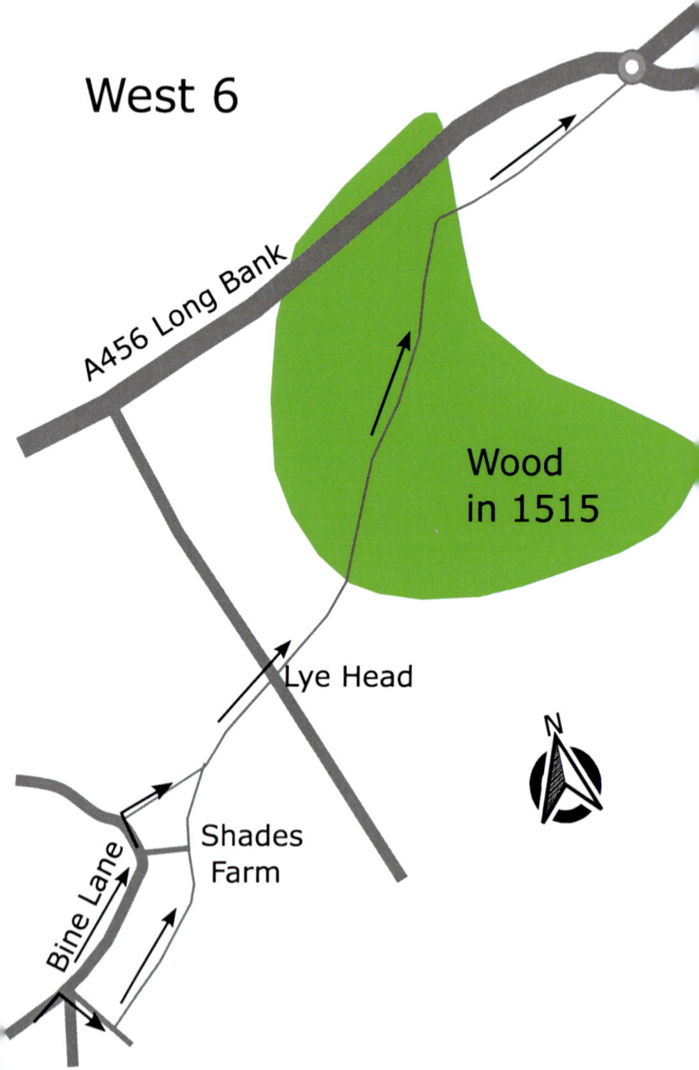

Turn right and then after a short distance turn left onto Bine Lane. [See Map West 6] Go up the Lane to the point roughly where the houses peter out. You have probably been on the route of the old 'wayne way' up to this point, but it has been disrupted and from here there are two possible routes to gain access back onto the old 'wayne way'.

The first route is to continue along Bine Lane, past Bine Farm and the entrance to Shades Farm. The lane bears left and dips down to a sharp left bend and a stream. There is a public footpath sign on the left and a public bridleway sign on the right. Turn right to follow the bridleway, but you immediately meet a challenge – a stream with no footbridge! There is a plastic pipe which can be used to get across without getting your feet wet unless the stream is in flood; the horses, of course, have no problem. You come up to a gate. Go through and bear right across the field and you will come onto the holloway; the footpath is marked as going diagonally across the field to join the holloway further up. (See the picture on the front cover)

The other route is to leave Bine Lane before the top of the hill (Orchard Close is on the left) where another lane joins and turn right along a trackway (to the left of the tarmacked road) following a sign which says the path is suitable for horses and cyclists as well as walkers. Go past a couple of houses and then you will see a stile on the left, just before an ivy-covered telegraph pole and the trackway turning to serve a red brick house. This stile is easy to climb over, but the one ahead of you is very difficult. Once in the field beyond, head slightly left down into the dip, then bear right up across the field, keeping the central shrub/tree on your right and you will come to a gate in the hedge. Go through and continue straight ahead through four more gates and then suddenly the area widens out. This may be part of the old 'wayne way'. You walk past Shades Farm (on your right), across its drive and through another gate (marked 'Bridle path'). This is clearly an old route. You come down to a ford for the horse riders, but there is a bridge for walkers. You are now in the holloway.

Neither of these routes is an easy walk and once you are in the holloway, you are faced with a muddy walk as horses churn up the soft soil. Trees line the route and you can imagine old wagons trundling up and down here – well, you can try; they wouldn't manage it nowadays!

At the top of the holloway is a gate. Go through this to continue on the old trackway. It passes some buildings on the right and then comes down to the road at Lye Head.

Cross this road and go slightly to your left to take the tarmacked lane to Coppice Gate Farm, passing the premises constructing Malvern sheds on the right. At the top of the slope there is a very clear indicator that you bear left to go along a footpath ('no horses, no cyclists') and into the wood rather than bearing right to go to the farmhouse. You pass some glasshouses on your left and enter the wood through a kissing gate. You are now in the area marked as Park on the 1515 map. As you enter the woodland, listen out for birdsong and you may see Fallow Deer.

There is a path off to your left, but go straight ahead where you soon take the left fork. The old map shows the road as straight, but we cannot be sure that the existing path is exactly on its line, though it can't be far off. It winds through the holly and other trees and then comes out into an area cleared for electricity lines. To your left you will catch a glimpse of the white water tower situated on Long Bank. Go straight over. There is often a lot of water in this area and the path can be very muddy. This trackway through the wood is a distinct holloway in places.

You emerge into an area where some new houses have been built and there is a neighbourhood watch system in place. You go round a gate and onto a trackway and are soon on a tarmacked drive. Walk up this past Bramblings on your left and Whiteoaks on your right (amongst others). You will get a view of the golf course and also a footpath off to your right, but keep going until you come to a bamboo fence, where there is a metal gate on your right.

The drive you have been on would take you out onto Long Bank by the former St Mary's Church. It may be that there was a route which continued the other side of Long Bank, going through what is now the grounds of Beaucastle to Uncllys and ultimately north to Buttonoak, but there is no through path there now. So we are going down into Bewdley.

Once through the gate, turn left to follow the path, well away from the golf balls (you hope!). This is a pretty woodland path in places and will take you right down to Wharton Park golf club, but there is some evidence of a holloway to your left for part of this path especially near an old oak tree (a blue pipe is laid through part of it) and that could well have been the original route. When you leave the car park, follow the driveway out to the bypass island. You can now follow the route into Bewdley described in Walk West 2.

The Whitty Pear

The Whitty Pear, *Sorbus domestica* (True Service Tree) is a very rare tree in Britain. Its usual home is in mainland Europe. One was found growing in the Wyre Forest in 1678 and celebrated, but botanists were puzzled by its presence At one time it was thought to be the only example in Britain, but others have now been identified, for example, along the cliffs of south Glamorgan and in the Wye valley.

The fruits are small. It has been suggested that it was not grown as a source of food, but perhaps as a tree of protection.

Rosemary's photo of the Whitty Pear

No obvious ancient trackway passes near our Whitty Pear, grid ref. SO749751. The current tree is a direct descendant of the original one. There is some evidence in the area for a dwelling a very long time ago and also some other, more nourishing, fruit bushes. If there was a tiny place here, perhaps the intention was to be ‘off the beaten track’.

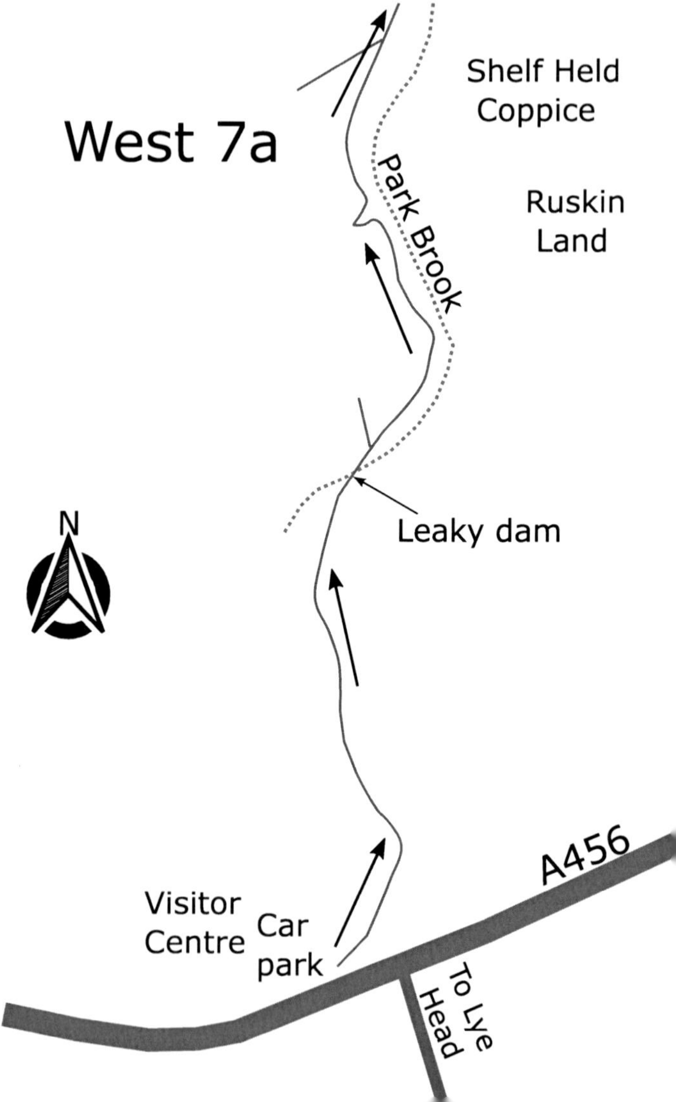
West 7a
Shelf Held
Coppice
Park Brook
Ruskin
Land
N
Leaky dam
A456
Visitor
Centre
Car
park
To Lye
Head

West 7 – Wyre Forest Visitor Centre to Buttonoak – 2¾ miles

Starting in the big car park at the Visitor Centre, head for the corner that is nearest to Bewdley, within sight of the main road, and you will pick up a track going north. On the other side of the A456 is the road to Lye Head. It looks as though there ought to be a continuation of that road on the northern side of the A456, but all evidence for that has been lost. The route that is about to be described may have been, in parts, an ancient route, linking a major ridgeway (the A456) with the Clun-Clee ridgeway at Buttonoak. Even if such a route never existed, this is still a lovely walk. [West 7a]

This track is used by horses, a marker post says 'Horse Trail Loop 1'; beyond it are visible the buildings of the Bewdley

Business Park. The first part of the track can be muddy and churned up by the hooves of the horses, but after a while you come down onto the road through the forest. This is a broad trackway with a good surface, so no mud in sight – at this point!

Look out for the nests of wood ants; they love areas that are open to the sunlight as they need the warmth. These insects are important recyclers of dead insects and predators of some Forest pests. During the warmer parts of the year they may be seen climbing trees where they feed on honeydew produced by aphids. Do not disturb them because they will retaliate by spraying formic acid, but they will do you no harm if you view them from a distance.

This is also the Arboretum Trail, the longest designated walk from the Visitor Centre. You follow it for some distance. The early part is also the Giants Trail.

Park Brook passes underneath the track. There used to be a pool to the left, but it has now silted up. On the right-hand side is a notice about Natural Flood Management and leaky dams.

There used to be more conifers in this area, but many have been felled and native oak woodland is being allowed to grow on. However, there is little in the way of undergrowth and small shrubs because much of the woodland has been shaded and young shoots are eaten by mammals.

The government decreed some years back that PAWS woodland (Plantations on Ancient Woodland Sites) should be reverted to native deciduous trees which are much better for a variety of wildlife. Many of our conifers planted post First World War were originally imported from abroad, for example, Douglas Fir from America, so our native wildlife has not had time to adapt and flourish on these trees. All of Wyre is classed as ancient woodland and so the conifer is now being removed over time.

Where the roadway divides, take the right-hand turning; the left-hand turning is marked as taking people back to the Visitor

Centre. You soon find yourself walking parallel to Park Brook, which is down to your right in a valley, the other side of which is very steep. Park Brook marks the boundary between the parish of Bewdley and the parish of Far Forest. On the Bewdley side is Shelf Held Coppice and Ruskin Land. The rock is exposed on the steep side and as some lime-rich water has flowed down from the springs above, so tufa has been formed in a few places.

In some parts along this route, fences have been erected in the past to allow the smaller trees and shrubs to get established; they show up now as areas where all the trees are young and of a similar height.

You will see the occasional sign for 'Horse Trail Loop 1' and that the track is suitable for cyclists.

[Move on to Map West 7b]

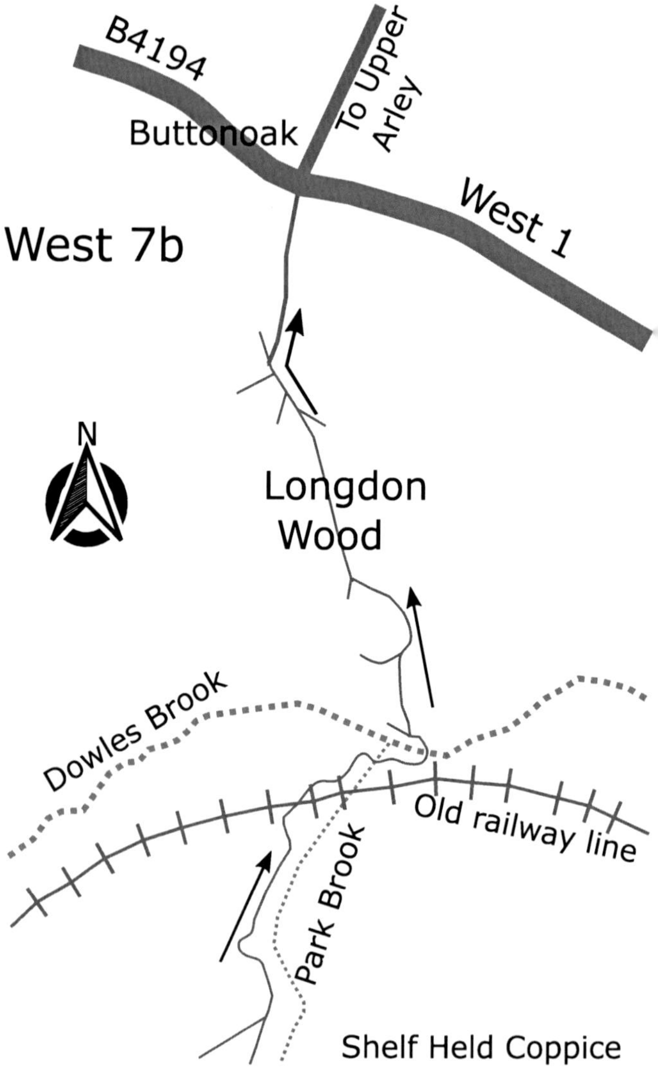
B4194
To Upper Arley
Buttonoak
West 1
West 7b
N
Longdon Wood
Dowles Brook
Old railway line
Park Brook
Shelf Held Coppice

A track comes in from the left which has a notice to say you are entering a sensitive wildlife area; actually, you aren't because you are taking the right-hand turning which takes you down to the old railway line. There is a sign post which says Bewdley is 2¼ miles to the right and Buttonoak is 3 miles to the left; this is for cyclists as well as walkers. Before you cross the old railway line, look to your left and you will see a notice board about butterflies in the forest. There is a convenient seat nearby if required for a break and a snack.

Cross the railway line and take the path marked 'Dowles Brook'. You very quickly come to a right turn down a somewhat narrow and muddy path towards the valley bottom. When you reach Dowles Brook, turn right to walk alongside it. Dippers,

Grey Wagtails and Kingfishers may be seen along the stream.

On your right, high up at the top of the hill, are some old planted conifers; these are not native to Wyre, but may provide a nesting site for Ravens which are often heard nearby. Ignore the paths off to the right and keep walking alongside the Brook. This can be muddy, as the photo shows. You are now faced by Park Brook as it comes in from the right, but, in low water, it is easily crossed using some stepping stones. A little further on there is a bridge over Dowles Brook; years ago there was a ford here, so this might have been a significant crossing place of Dowles Brook, which marks the county boundary between Worcestershire and Shropshire. Cross over and walk up to the junction. To your right you will see the buildings of Coopers Mill. Turn left to walk up the hill.

You come to a fork in the trackway. The most direct route is to turn right and continue up the hill where you bear right again at the top of the slope.

This is a pleasant walk through Longdon Wood where, again, efforts have been made to reduce the number of conifers and allow native deciduous trees to flourish. You may see cattle owned by the Wyre Community Land Trust. These have been trained to stay within an invisible fence, the boundary of which is controlled from the office by satellite! They help to manage the woodland. You pass on your left a wooden pen for use with the cattle.

At the edge of the wood, you come to a fork in the trackway; take the right-hand road. This is tree lined and looks more like an ancient route. You will see a gate ahead; you can walk round the side of this. In the pasture field to your right among the mole hills are also mounds created by Yellow Meadow Ants. You are nearing civilisation! You walk past a few dwellings and other buildings and come to the B4194. This is the Clun-Clee ridgeway (see Walk West 1) so a very ancient route. Ahead of you is the road to Pound Green and a direct route to Upper Arley and an important crossing of the Severn.

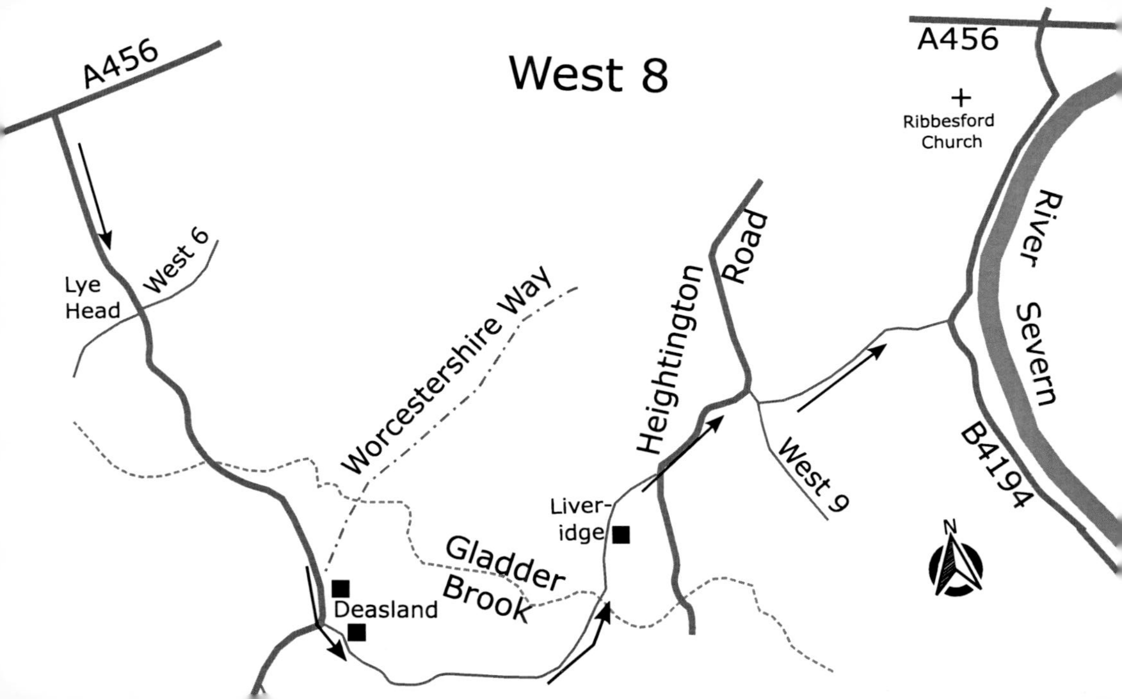
West 8
A456
A456
Ribbesford
Church
River Severn
B4194
Road
Heightington
West 9
West 6
Lye
Head
Worcestershire Way
Liver-
idge
Gladder
Brook
Deasland
N

West 8 – Wyre Forest Visitor Centre to Bewdley via Deasland – 8 miles

The turning off the A456 to Lye Head could be an ancient route. We suggested that Walk 7 could be a continuation of that road on the northern side of the A456. Lye Head Road goes south through Cross Bank and on to Lye Head before continuing down to Deasland Farm where it crosses the Worcestershire Way.

The Worcestershire Way was created as a long-distance footpath in 1989. In some places, it almost certainly follows old paths and this is the case here. The route northeast which crosses Little Lakes golf course is on the line of an old footpath. When the Way reaches the road near Horsehill Farm, it soon diverges off to go through the woods above Ribbesford

Church, but perhaps the road, known as Light Lane, was an old trackway. Shortly after crossing the bypass, there is a footpath off to the left which goes down the hill to the Golden Valley; this used to be a marked holloway, but has been ploughed out and is now occupied by Dexter cattle. The Way is rejoined at the bottom of this hill.

Back on the Lye Head road, Deasland Farm is on your left and there is a modern timber framed house on your right. A little further on the road swings right, but take the track to the left by the farm buildings to find another holloway.

If you had kept on the road, it would have taken you down through, in part, a holloway to the Heightington road and the ridgeway described in Walk West 4. Thus it is possible to pursue a route all the way from Upper Arley via Pound Green and the

Forest to reach Heightington and then on to Dunley and beyond.

Back in the entrance to the Deasland cow sheds, there is a gate beside which is a small gate for pedestrians and also a footpath sign with a reminder to keep your dog on a lead. [Map West 8] Go through and then bear right onto the higher level (covered with moss) by a cow shed with machinery in it. Bear right round the end of the shed and there is a trackway ahead of you. This turns into a holloway bounded by tall trees and can be VERY muddy. Follow this up the hill to where the trees end. Pause to enjoy the view: to your right you can see across to the main Heightington road and hidden in the trees (between the white house and the silo) is St Giles' church.

Go through the small gate (next to a large one) and continue straight ahead through this grassy field, with the hedge on your right. You will come to a gate on your right, again with views to the south. There is a stile over the barbed wire, but this leads to a route that is not officially recognised, so ignore it unless you want a better photograph of the lime tree. This amazing tree is staring you in the face.

Years ago many lime trees were pollarded (cut above the height of browsing animals). The regrowth was often harvested in late summer and dried to provide winter fodder for farm animals.

Go through the small gate to the left of the lime tree and follow the track with the hedge on your left. You will eventually come to a gap in the hedge ahead of you. Go through and you will see there is a clear path down the hill, past an oak tree and into the valley.

At the bottom of the hill is Gladder Brook over which there is a bridge. A tributary runs into the Brook at this point, so this is a pretty dingle. The path wanders up through the trees to come out at the edge of Liveridge Farm. The route is very clear until you get into the yard where there is a red brick wall. Bear left round the shed and cross the wide expanse of concrete to follow the driveway giving access to Liveridge Farm, which consists nowadays of eight dwellings.

Walk along the driveway. There used to be a path slightly to the right, but this has been lost. Where you reach a footpath marker going off to the left is the point where the old path came in from the right. The path to the left goes across to Park End and beyond. Perhaps that is where this path originally went, but we are heading for Bewdley, so continue to the end of the driveway. This is Heightington Road. Turn left; this is a narrow road, so beware of traffic.

The road does a very sharp left-hand turn by an entrance into the woodland. On the corner facing you is Glebe Cottage. Turn right, walk round the barrier and a large notice will tell you that this is Ribbesford Wood. Very soon going off this wide track there is a narrow path on the left. Follow this down the valley; you will pass a huge wood ants' nest on your left. Go straight over the forestry track and continue in a straight line until you come to the forestry track again. Here, bear right along the forestry track and continue on it down the hill until the track peters out and you see a fork in the path above the mobile home park.

If we are on the line of an ancient route, we would probably have gone straight ahead and down to the river. The Wallbrook shoal is just across the football pitch, while the Ribbesford Shoal is less than half a mile to the north. There are no obvious trackways on the other side of either of these shoals.

For the purpose of completing a journey to Bewdley, you will need to follow the main road and then keep to the riverside once the road turns up the hill near the Blackstone Country Park. However, above the mobile home park, there is a footpath marked going left, but this soon goes uphill through the woodland. There is an obvious path following the contours all the way to Ribbesford churchyard, but this is not an official path.

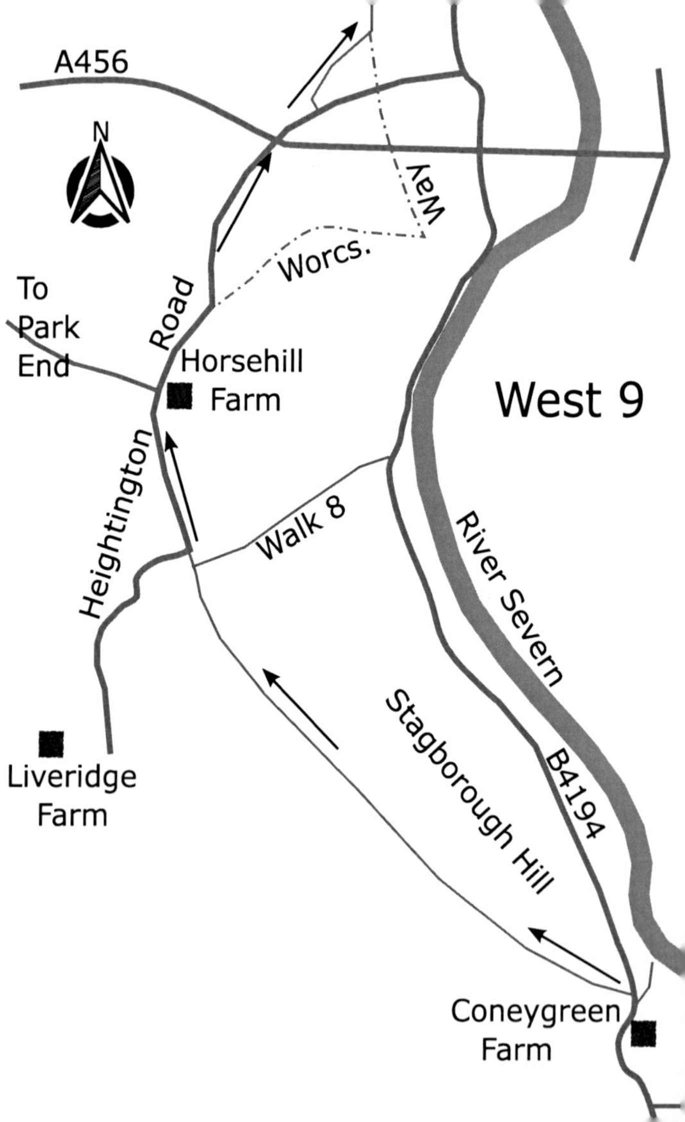
A456
N
To
Park
End
Road
Worcs.
Way
Horsehill
Farm
West 9
Heightington
Walk 8
River Severn
Stagborough Hill
B4194
Liveridge
Farm
Coneygreen
Farm

West 9 – Coneygreen to Bewdley via Stagborough Hill – 5 miles

Near Coneygreen Farm, there is a layby on the B4194 at SO795714 and there is a very clear holloway going down to the river. This might have linked with the Lickhill shoal and provided a route across the river at that point. So perhaps travellers came from Mitton (now Stourport) via Lickhill to cross the Severn and then came up the holloway to get onto our route over Stagborough. [Map West 9]

We begin our walk by crossing the road and climbing a stile by a footpath notice. Keep the fence on your left and part way up the field there is a kissing gate which you go through. You are now faced with climbing up the hill. There are several routes as this area has been used for motor racing. At the top all the tracks converge to form a wide sandy track with a hedge on the left and gorse on the right. Walk up here until you come to the remains of a large tree trunk. There is a stile on the left, but there is also a gap in the fence so you can walk through.

Turn right and follow the track until you come to another open gate. This can be very wet here and there is a stile which you can use to avoid the mud. Continue along the track keeping close to the hedge on your left. To your right is Stagborough Hill itself on the top of which is a trig point.

Walk on for nearly half a mile and then you will see a kissing gate on your left which will take you away from the open land and into the wood. For a short distance there is a wire fence on your right. Then the track widens out. This is a clear straight road and you keep on it all the way, ignoring any turnings to the right or the left. You are actually walking along a ridgeway although it is difficult to see this with so many trees. You will pass an area on your right where trees have been cleared. These have been replaced with a mixture of species, currently protected with plastic tubes to stop them being eaten. You may notice some nests of wood ants in the sunny patches along this route. Eventually you come to a metal barrier marking the end of the wood. You cross Walk West 8 at this point.

You come out onto Heightington Road by Glebe Cottage. The road goes left to Liveridge Farm, but our route is straight ahead. Continue on the road and note it is ridgeway with good views. You pass a left-hand turn to the Frank Chapman Centre at Park End; Horsehill Farm is on your right. You are now on the Worcestershire Way. Where the Way bears off right into woodland, keep on the road down past the tracks to Haye Farm and to Park Farm (both on your left) and over the bypass.

Just after a lay-by near 'Phoenix Land' is a path off to the left. After a short distance along it, you will see a way through the fence on your right which takes you down the hill. As already mentioned, there was once a holloway through this area, but it has been ploughed out. You pass through a gate in a hedge and then another gate to come onto the path that leads to Ribbesford. You are back on the Worcestershire Way and can turn left to follow the signs back into Bewdley.

A thought: If a traveller was at Gilgal and wanted to get to Bewdley, then the obvious way would have been to go over Burlish Top (Walk East 9). However, by going across to the Lickhill shoal and getting onto the Stagborough route, the traveller might then have been able to get access via Liveridge to Deasland and go either due north (on Walks West 8 and then 7) or go across to Lane End Farm and get on a ridgeway (Walk West 4) which links with the other ridgeway to Clows Top (Walk West 2). So many possibilities!

West 10

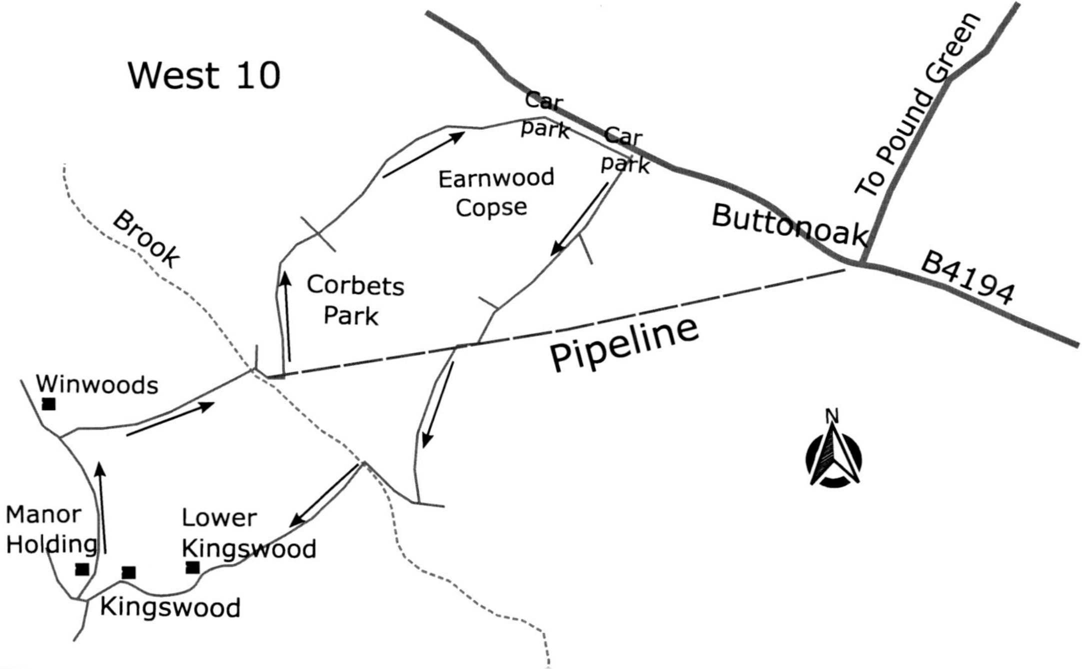
To Pound Green
B4194
Buttonoak
Car park
Car park
Earnwood Copse
Corbets Park
Pipeline
Brook
N
Winwoods
Manor Holding
Lower Kingswood
Kingswood

West 10 – A circular walk from Buttonoak via Kingswood – 3½ miles

This walk is inspired by the fact that there are what appear to be ancient trackways, but it is not obvious how they fit with others that we suggest. It can be enjoyed as a circular walk which involves no made-up roads at all, but watch out for mud if the weather has been wet. [See Map West 10]

Start at the small car park on the left-hand side of the B4194 just after you leave the restricted area of Buttonoak, going north. The grid reference, for those who like these, is SO746782. Cross the brook and ahead of you is a very clear bridle path and a sign which says 'Horse Trail Loop 2'. There is also a finger post which reads 'Bewdley 5¼ miles, Callow Hill Visitor Centre 3¾ miles'. After about half a mile there is a path off to the left and you may catch a glimpse of a notice board along it, which you may want to go and read. It has been erected by Natural England. There is a boundary here between the area cared for by the Forestry Commission and that cared for by Natural England. Our suggested route keeps to the bridle path, the Horse Trail Loop 2, on the Forestry Commission land. The track sides are mowed in winter to restrict the growth of bracken and allow flowering plants like bluebells to flourish.

Further on, a track comes in from the right, but the signpost points left. It reads 'Bewdley 4¼ miles, Callow Hill Visitor Centre 3¼ miles'. It also has the 45 cycle path notice. So, go left and soon you will come to an open area which stretches to the left and to the right. This is the route of the Elan Valley water pipeline; it is kept clear of trees for the purpose of access. Turn right along its route. The ground is somewhat soggy here and people joke that the pipe is leaking! You will see a marker post some 200 or so yards away. Turn left when you reach it, down a seriously muddy pathway. Keep going downhill, ignoring a pathway coming in from the right and other small paths to right and left; continue for some distance until you reach a T junction, which is near an old yew tree, but you may not spot that. There is a notice indicating that the path you have come down is part of Horse Trail Loop 2. Turn right on to the narrower path and follow it down to the brook, ignoring any paths which may entice you away. There are many different mosses and liverworts along the sides of this damp trackway.

At the bottom you come to a stile. Climb over that and then cross over the brook using the footbridge, although there is a ford if you fancy trying that. You then come up through the trees and out into an open meadow. In the spring this is yellow with cowslips. In the top corner of the field is a metal kissing gate; head for that and go through it.

You are now on what appears to be an ancient trackway. It is wide with hedges on either side. There is at least one old map which shows a road from here back to Buttonoak, but that might be a map maker's imagination as, clearly, the track you have taken is a more modern creation. However, the existence of this section of old trackway suggests there was once some kind of route, perhaps through to Buttonoak. Continue up the trackway, over a stile and then through another kissing gate. You are now close to Lower Kingswood, the garden and house being on the right. You come out onto a lane at the entrance to Lower Kingswood. The trackway curves round to the left and then comes back, creating almost a semi-circle; it appears to be respecting an ancient boundary. It is believed there was an Iron Age settlement at Lower Kingswood; this was mentioned in Walk West 5.

So, bear left to follow the lane, past a pond on your right and then between the buildings which formed Kingswood Farm; there are several dwellings here. After the gated entrance to a house on your left, you will see the route into the forest mentioned in Walk West 5. Ignore that and take the turning on the right which leads to Manor Holding. This lane passes the building (on the left) and then becomes a narrow path with not only a public footpath notice but also a Geopark Way sign. Follow that and you come out through a kissing gate into a field. Keep to the hedgeline and eventually go through another kissing gate and field before finding an open track on the left (which leads to Winwoods) and a stile over the fence directly in front of you.

Climb over the stile and turn right to walk down this wide, grassy area right down to the brook you crossed earlier. At one point, you pass through a wide gap in the hedge. Within the hedge to your left, there seems to be the remains of a holloway, but it is completely impassable.

You are walking more or less along the route of the Elan Valley water pipeline and you will see some of the pipework at the bottom of the valley. When you reach the bottom, the path you need is slightly to the left, where you will find a footbridge over the brook. Once over, take the right-hand path up into the open area. You can look down on the engineering work associated with the pipeline and even go down for a closer look, though take care. The first two pipes from the Elan Valley were laid over a hundred years ago, the pipeline being opened in 1904 by Edward VII. A third pipe was added in 1939 and a fourth in 1961.

Walk left, up the hill, for a short distance. Do not go as far as the very steep part of the path. Over to your left is the enticing entrance to a holloway which will amaze you. It is wide, well defined and runs for a long way up towards the main road, the B4194.

The area is known as Corbets Park and is planted with beech trees under which little thrives because of the dense shade. Only a short way up the holloway, there is on the left evidence that some of the stone has been quarried out, perhaps for use in the structure you have seen by the brook.

The holloway eventually peters out and there is simply an ordinary path. The line of the holloway might well continue, but it is difficult to see. The path bears right and soon crosses a wide track. There is a post at the junction, on the back of which is a 'Horse Trail Loop 2' notice. You are now going to follow the Horse Trail right back to the car park.

As you walk up the track straight ahead of you, look out for the nests of wood ants. You might also see them making trails up trees in order to reach the aphids which they milk for their honeydew, a source of food.

After wending your way through the woodland you will eventually come out onto a wider track by a gate and a car park. A notice there will tell you about Earnwood Copse. To complete the circle back to the other car park, you need to take the pathway by the notice board and keep to the wooden fence, as you walk parallel to the main road and come back to where you started.

Crossing the Severn

On the next two pages are maps of the River Severn with the shallow areas known as shoals marked. Those below Bewdley appear on a map of 1803[8] with their names. Those above Bewdley have been identified by local people who have named them.

---

[8] WAAS BA338 ref. 161/4

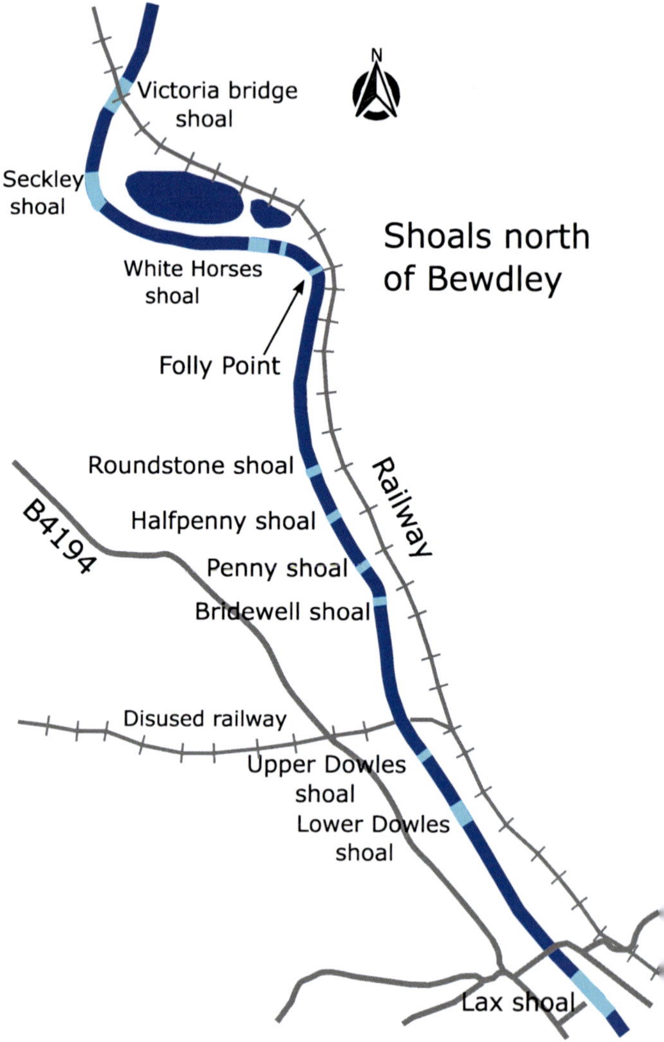

N
Shoals north of Bewdley
Victoria bridge shoal
Seckley shoal
White Horses shoal
Folly Point
Roundstone shoal
Halfpenny shoal
Penny shoal
Bridewell shoal
Railway
B4194
Disused railway
Upper Dowles shoal
Lower Dowles shoal
Lax shoal

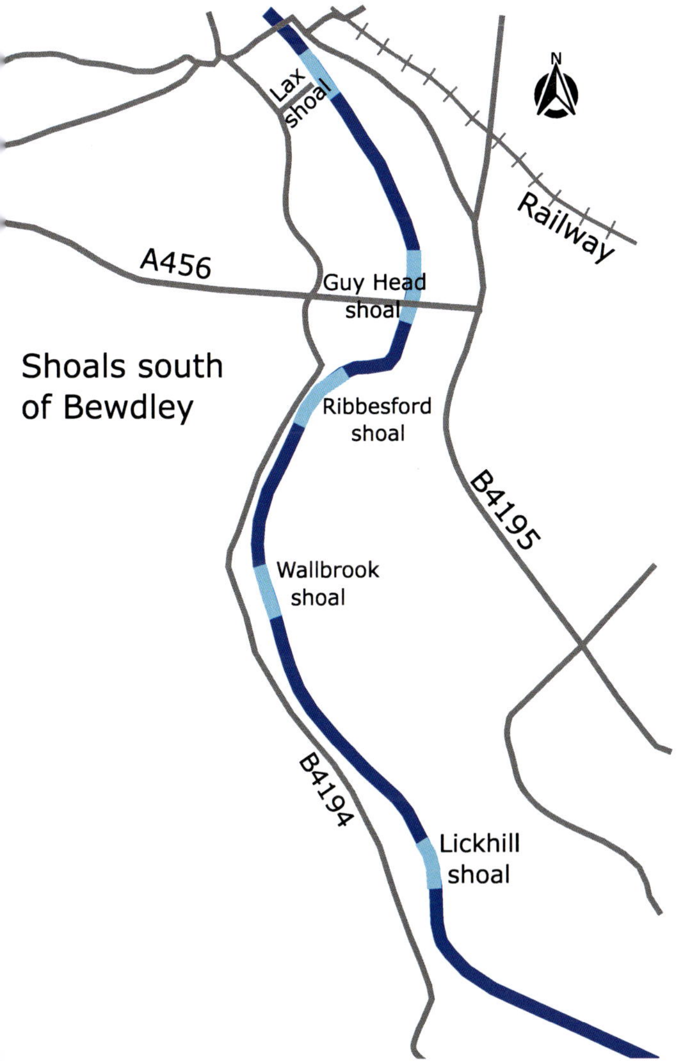
Shoals south of Bewdley
N
Lax shoal
Railway
A456
Guy Head shoal
Ribbesford shoal
B4195
Wallbrook shoal
B4194
Lickhill shoal

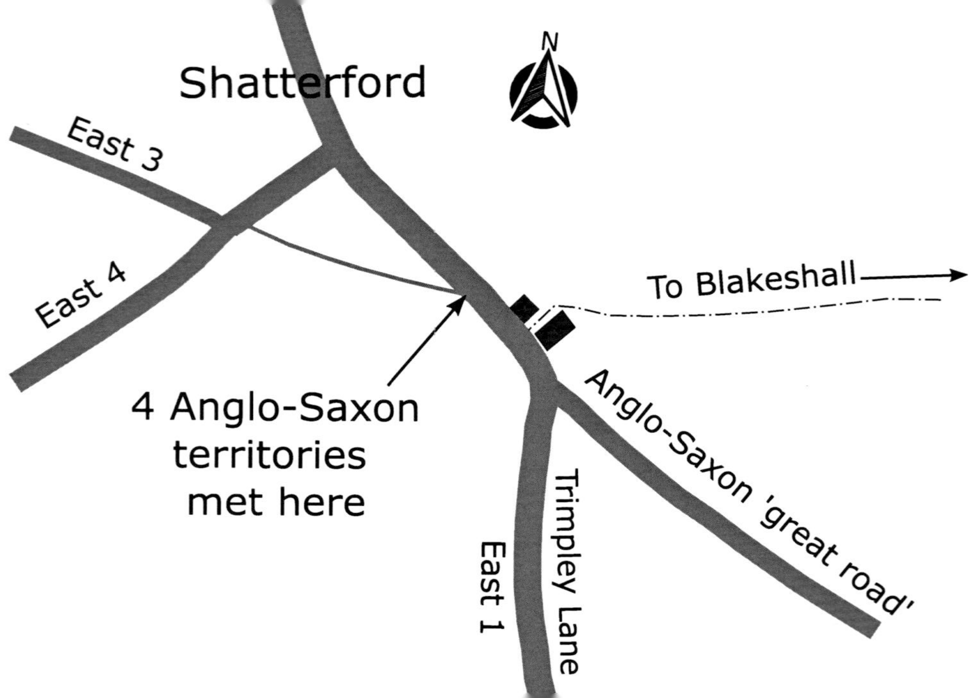
Shatterford
N
East 3
East 4
To Blakeshall
4 Anglo-Saxon territories met here
Anglo-Saxon 'great road'
Trimpley Lane
East 1

East 1 – Shatterford to Northwood Lane – 3¼ miles

There is a special place at Shatterford which appears unremarkable, but is actually a meeting place of four Anglo-Saxon territories. [See map] The grid reference is SO792807, where a footpath crosses Trimpley Lane. The footpath goes up the side of a cottage and then turns due east along the line of a hedge and heads across to Blakeshall. (This can be walked, but with great difficulty.)

Nearby is the North Worcestershire Path (formerly the Worcestershire Way), which follows the road east past Upper Birch Farm and then has to turn north to link up with a more direct route to Blakeshall.

A charter dated AD866 refers to a 'great road',[9] clearly an ancient route, which must be the tarmacked road. Grundy calls it Route 51.

You may notice that there is a plain stone set by the wall near the footpath to Blakeshall, outside Bank Cottage. This has

[9] Della Hooke, *Worcestershire Anglo-Saxon Charter Bounds* (Studies in Anglo- Saxon History II, 1990), pp. 121-125

no marking, so seems unlikely to have been a mile stone. Perhaps it indicated the old boundary between Staffordshire and Worcestershire which ran along the Blakeshall path, crossed the road by the stone and then ran down through Eymore Wood slightly to the south of the North Worcestershire Path.

This place is not only a meeting place of territories, but also seems to be a meeting place of trackways. Mention has already been made of the two going east. Other routes lead off from this significant meeting place. The existing tarmacked road going north must be one of them; it joins up with the A442 at Bellmans Cross in Shatterford. Another might have led down to the crossing of the Severn at Upper Arley (see Walk East 3) and another to a crossing of the Severn close to Folly Point (see Walk

East 4). There is also Trimpley Lane itself which goes south; it is a ridgeway track which Grundy calls Route 65 and we have called East 1.

The tarmacked road (Trimpley Lane) goes due south (with a few kinks) for about a mile. You come to a right-hand turning for Trimpley reservoir and church. [See Map East 1a] Just past this turning, there should be a track off to the right. There is indeed a footpath notice on the side of the main road, but this leads nowhere! The path seems to have been lost, so you need to go down the road a little further to find the driveway (on the right) which leads to Bite Farm. On the way down the drive, you will see a stile and a footpath going off to the right; this cuts across to the Trimpley reservoir road.

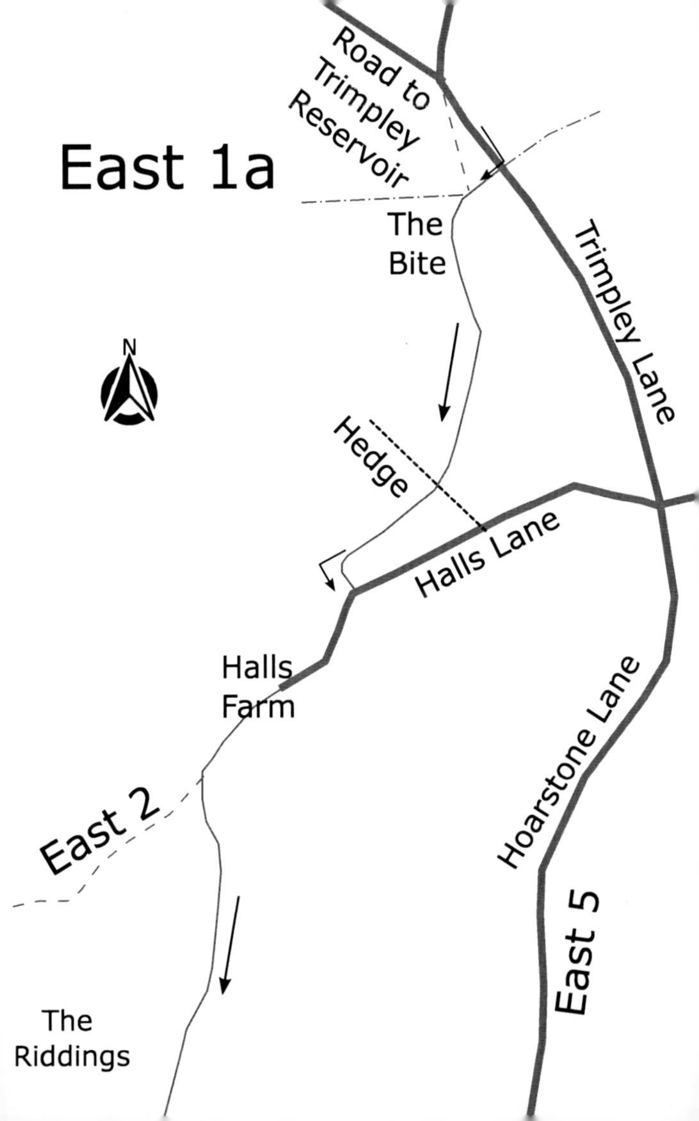
East 1a
Road to Trimpley Reservoir
The Bite
N
Trimpley Lane
Hedge
Halls Lane
Halls Farm
Hoarstone Lane
East 2
East 5
The Riddings

As you approach the farm buildings, you need to bear left to a gate which takes you into a field. Bear right across the field to find a stile and then straight over the next field to find another gate. You are heading for Halls Farm Lane; there are two possibilities. One is to continue more or less straight on to a wide gate (which may be open) and directly onto the lane. The other (and probably the official path) is to bear right to find a stile in the hedge line where there are some large trees (there is a pylon a little further to the right). Once over the stile, you follow the boundary along the back of some houses, before turning sharp left to go down a wide track to the lane. The advantage of this second route is that there are some glorious views of the countryside out to the west.

Once on Halls Lane, whichever way you have taken, turn right and follow the lane until you reach the farm. Where the hard surfaced road goes down into the farmyard, take the muddier track to the right, at the higher level. It turns right and then left and goes down between an open barn on your right and a brick barn on your left. There is a bridle path notice on the left-hand side. You are on a track with old machinery either side of you, but beautiful views all around. Straight ahead of you, at the bottom of the field, is a gate marked 'Private Property Keep Out'. You need to veer off to the left to go through a gate marked with a bridle path notice. This path can be muddy. (It is described going in the other direction in 'Walking Bewdley's History' where it is Walk 9.)

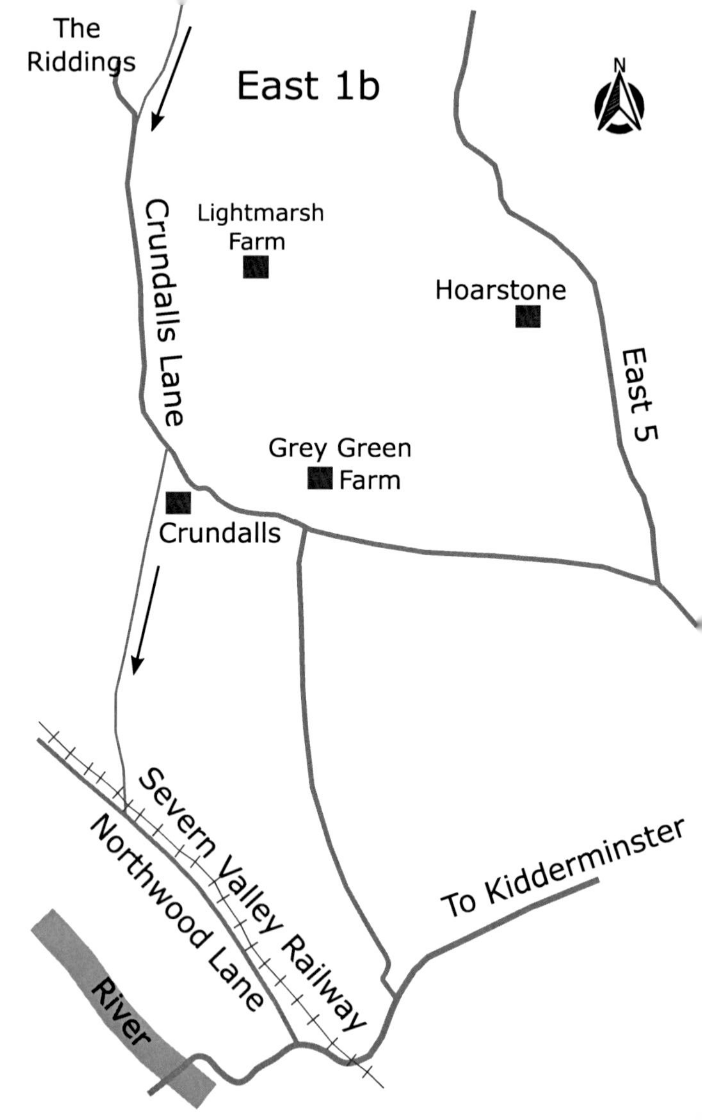

The Riddings
East 1b
N
Lightmarsh Farm
Hoarstone
Crundalls Lane
East 5
Grey Green Farm
Crundalls
Severn Valley Railway
Northwood Lane
To Kidderminster
River

On the other side of the gate, follow the path keeping the hedge on your left. You then go into another field, but this time there is a wire fence on your right and the hedge on your left. In some 1869 sales particulars for Halls Farm, this is described as the road to Bewdley! Eventually the path passes between hedges and you come out onto a track. [Move on to Map East 1b] There are several properties in this area, so the track is suitable now for vehicles. A little further on you pass, on your right, the entrance to The Riddings.

You are now on Crundalls Lane. Follow this for about half a mile. There is a cottage on your right and then the farm buildings of Crundalls Farm. Turn right up a tarmacked trackway, cross the cattle grid and then climb over the stile into the field. Follow the hedge on your left. Then bear left round the corner (the land falls away slightly in front of you) and head for the gate/stile. When you have passed through this, turn right to follow the pathway alongside the hedge. There is another stile before you come out into a field and bear slightly left to walk down the centre of this area. You will see the railway line ahead of you. There is a stile which will take you to a tunnel under the line and out onto Northwood Lane, where you turn left to make your way into Bewdley.

It is unclear where the ancient route went at this point. Perhaps it headed for the river to find a ford. Lizzie Hill of Bewdley Historical Research Group has a theory that the route crossed the river at what we have called Lower Dowles shoal and then went up in a straight line to Lakes Road and on to Wharton Park. Or perhaps the trackway passed along Northwood Lane and through Butt Town Meadow Caravan Park, as the path does today.

East 2 (inaccessible)

As you came through Halls Farm, you bore left and avoided the gate straight ahead of you, the one that is marked 'Private Property Keep Out'. That is not now a recognised footpath, but it is clearly shown on some old maps.

It followed the valley down, staying on the higher ground until it dropped down to Northwood Lane near Bridewell Cottage. The logic is that it was heading for a way across the Severn and this is indeed the site of an old ford, known locally as Penny Ford.

East 3

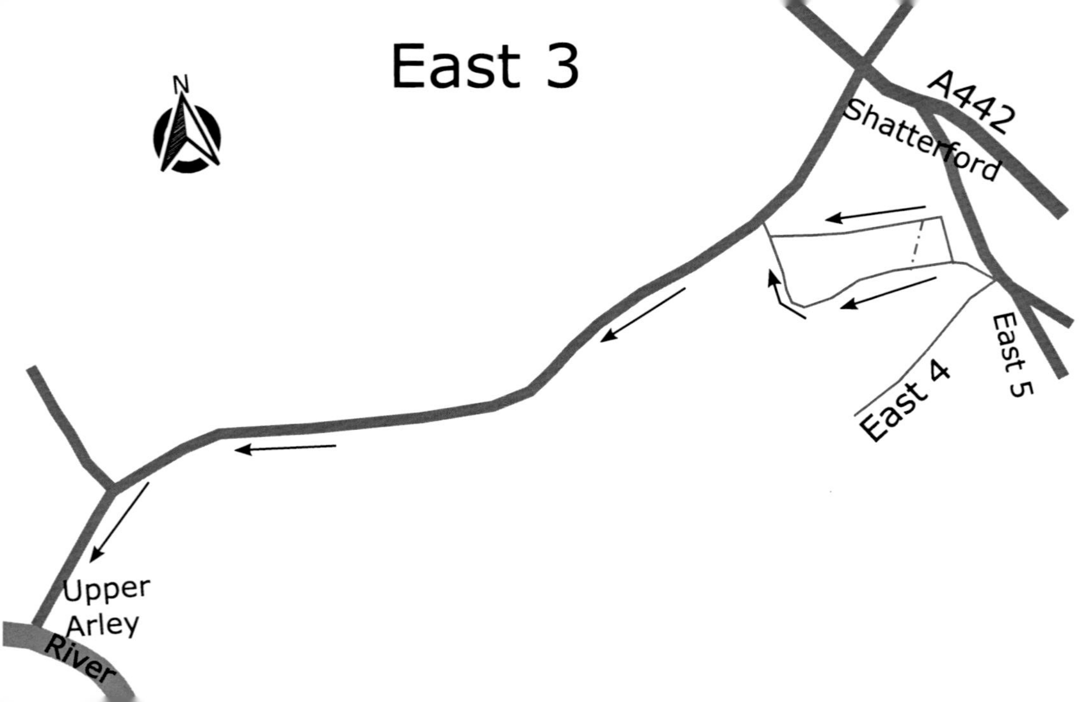

East 3 – Shatterford to Upper Arley – 2 miles

From the Anglo-Saxon meeting place, it was suggested that there was a way down to Upper Arley. [See Map East 3] A signpost points across the green area to the south of the road. The lane divides; take the right-hand fork (the route to the left follows the North Worcestershire Path). For a short distance the lane is wide, as it provides access to some properties. Then there is a narrow bridle way straight ahead over the grass and between the hedges. Follow this down a gentle slope.

You pass a dwelling on the right and also a path off to the right (see alternative route below), but continue straight on. Further down, the path passes a trackway on the right, a gate into a garden and a hedge as it bears slightly to the left before making a turn to the right where it goes through a deep holloway. In wet weather, this is very muddy and can even be a stream!

You eventually emerge from walking between holly trees onto a wider track which serves Holly Leaf Cottage and Hollies Farm. This track will take you through to the main road; opposite is a bus shelter with a seat and some houses.

There is an alternative to the muddy holloway. Take the path off to the right which is a wide trackway in front of a modern house. You soon reach the tarmacked drive to the house. Turn left for a short distance. The tarmacked road sweeps to the left, but the path continues straight ahead as a track between hedges, leading gently downwards. There is a path off to the right (with a beautiful view of Brown Clee hill) which leads back up to the main road, but continue on down the hill; it can be muddy here too, so take care. It is not really a holloway, but may be an ancient path.

You emerge onto an open place with hardcore. On the left is a metal gate and on the right a building. Keep walking straight ahead, past an extended house on the right and you will come onto the lane which leads right, up to the main road and the bus shelter.

Turn left to follow the main road down to the village of Upper Arley where there must have been an ancient crossing of the Severn. The earliest reference to a ferry at Upper Arley is in 1332.

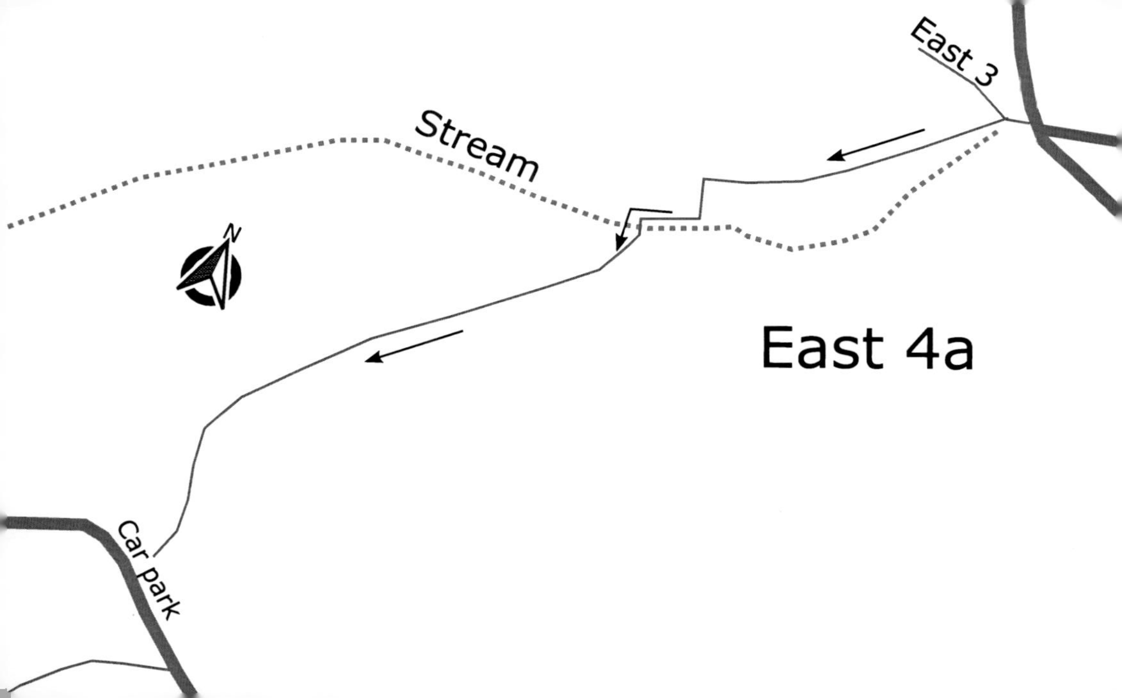

East 4a
East 3
Stream
Car park
N

East 4 – Shatterford to opposite Hawkbatch – 2 miles

Another route from the Anglo-Saxon meeting place is the North Worcestershire Path itself. This is obviously a modern name, but some of the trackway may follow an old route. [See Map East 4a] A signpost points across the green area to the south of the road. The lane divides; take the left-hand fork to follow the fir cone signs for the Path. The names on the (usually open) gate are Woodcot Deep and Deerhouse. Follow this wide track past these properties. After Deerhouse the trackway is rougher. You will come to a closed gate which you can walk round.

Continue to follow the track as it slowly descends through Eymore Wood. There are other trackways going off, but the fir cone signs should keep you on the right one. One of the posts with the North Worcestershire Path sign also has carved into it WW (see photo), which probably stands for Worcestershire Way, an earlier name for this path.

Over to your right, a deeper path runs parallel for some distance. This may be the remnants of an old holloway or may be a 'tushing' ditch created by horses pulling timber out of the woods. The trackway changes when you reach a kissing gate.

The other side of the gate is an open field and the path turns sharp left, being bounded on the right-hand side by barbed wire. If you were on an ancient route before, you aren't now! This path takes you along the edge of the field and down some steps before it turns sharp right to follow the stream, which is well below the level of the footpath, so do take care here as the path is narrow and slippery. The stream goes down to Worralls Mill, near Upper Arley village. There is more barbed wire on the right-hand side.

You come to a bridge over the stream. A trackway goes straight on, but the Path uses this bridge to cross over and then goes straight on up the hill. At the top it bears right and eventually comes up onto a wide trackway, where you turn right. Follow this for some distance, enjoying the sounds of the wood. After a while you reach a concrete bridge over a stream and there is a fir cone sign on the far side of the bridge.

In Walk West 7 it was mentioned that the government decreed some years back that PAWS woodland (Plantations on Ancient Woodland Sites) should be reverted to native deciduous trees which are much better for a variety of wildlife. There is a monetary incentive to do this, a relevant factor here as Eymore Wood is in private ownership.

Further on, up the top of a hill, there is a crossroads (SO 778795). The fir cone sign indicates that our path goes straight ahead, along a narrower path. A blue arrow points left and nothing is indicated to the right. A green arrow also points straight ahead. You now wind your way through woodland, some of which is fairly new and replaced conifers to create a more diverse wooded area. At a T junction, the fir cone and the green arrow both point right. You soon find a little wooden footbridge to take you over a stream. Straight ahead are some steps which lead into the car park.

[Move on to Map East 4b]

Exit the car park and take the road left for a short distance. You will see a track (marked footpath) off to the right; this leads to a gate where there is a stile to clamber over. Bear left through the field and then

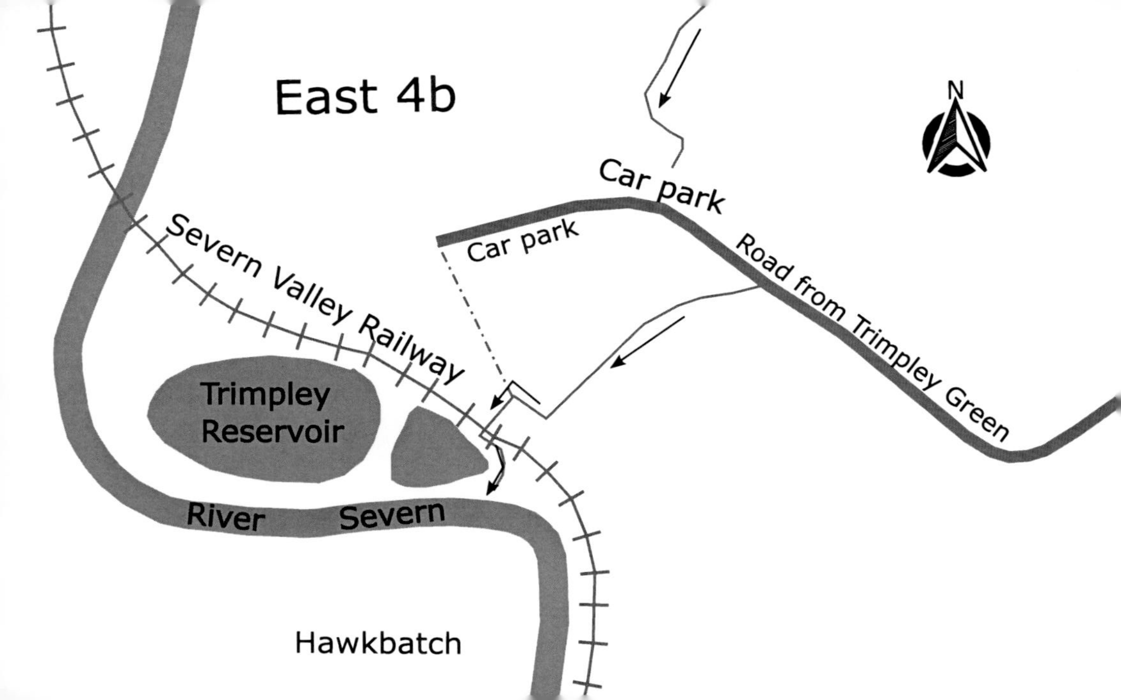

East 4b
N
Car park
Car park
Road from Trimpley Green
Severn Valley Railway
Trimpley Reservoir
River Severn
Hawkbatch

follow a hedgeline, walking straight ahead with the hedge on your right. You will come down the slope to a stile. You now enter the wood and before long you will find yourself following a holloway down towards the river. This looks like an ancient trackway and indeed may be one, but it does not go all the way to the Severn.

Part way down the hill, the holloway disappears and there is a gate on your left which leads to a cottage and you have to take the path which goes sharp right, down a dip and then up the hill (past the remnants of a quarry on your right), before you turn left to go down onto a wider trackway. Bear left to reach the Severn Valley Railway line; cross with care, as this line can be very busy at times.

You now have to follow the trackway left. This goes right to skirt the reservoir and you can soon bear left to go down to the river itself. Was there a crossing of the river at this point? It does not look very inviting! There is, however, a path heading southwest on the other side of the river.

A map of 1756[10] of the Eymore estate (see next page) shows the stream which comes down to the river at this point and names the field to the west of the stream as Field 1. The map also shows a building next to Field 1. The accompanying terrier calls Field 1 the 'Green Load Leasowe'.[11]

The next field to the west (Field 3) is called Twitchill Leasow and in the river is shown a small island at the point now known as White Horses Ford. Only a short distance west of this is an area of the Severn known as Forty Foot Drop or Claypits Deeps; the depth of water can be 40 feet even in the summer.

---

[10] WAAS BA5403/20 ref.b009:1

[11] WAAS BA2602/75 ref.009:1

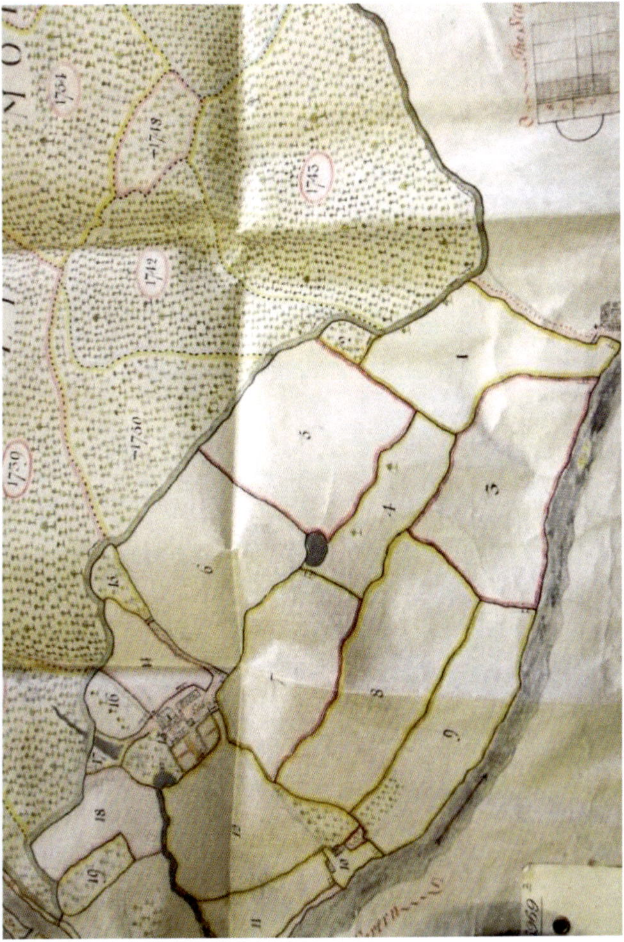

Map of Eymore estate in 1756
(North to the left)

The next field to the west (Field 9) is a long one called 'Leasow above the Load'; it is shown on more recent maps as 'liable to floods', but the banks have been raised in the last half century. Then there is a small field (Field 10) with a building which is 'Priors Load Cottage and garden'. The next field west (Field 11) is called 'Meadow above the Load'. 'Load' can sometimes be a corruption of 'lode' (OE *gelād*), which has the probable meaning of 'difficult river crossing' and possibly 'ferry' in several places on the Severn in Worcestershire and Gloucestershire.[12] So we have a stretch of land (about a quarter of a mile) to which was attached the word 'load'. In the river itself there is the ford and the very deep section of the river, so 'load' could be

---

[12] Margaret Gelling, *Place-names in the Landscape* (London, 1984), p. 75

related to crossing the river or the word could be being used in the more common way of loading boats with goods, in this case probably timber from the wood.

The terrain has been severely disrupted by the building of the Severn Valley Railway in 1861 and the Trimpley reservoir in 1964. On the other side is Hawkbatch, where modern chalets have been built on an ancient site. It seems likely there was a way across, but perhaps it was not a well-used ford.

A little further downriver there is an area with 'riffles' (when the water is low) indicating a shallow stretch of river and another one round the bend to the right which is known as Folly Point.

East 5a

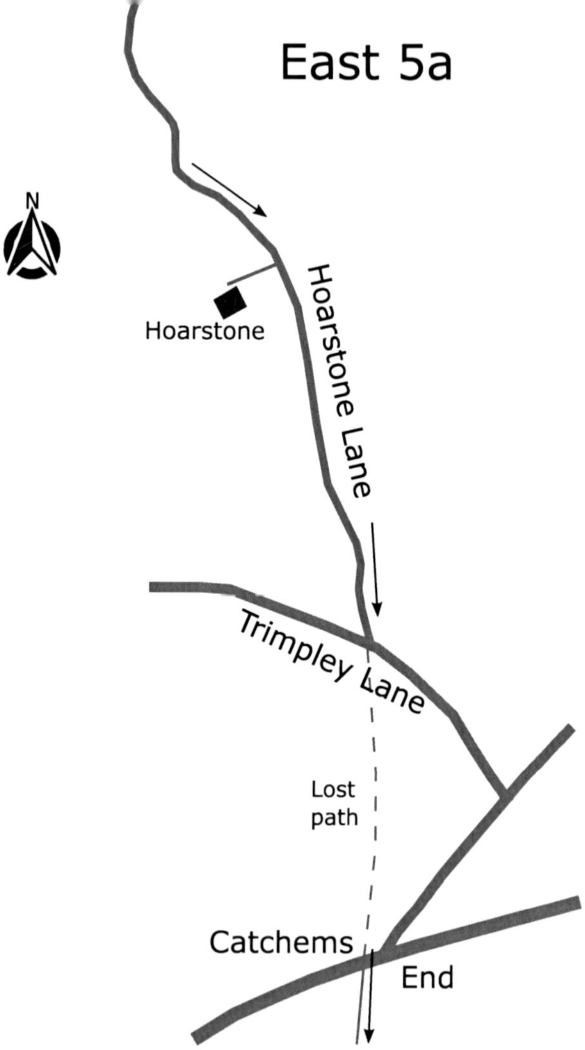
N
Hoarstone
Hoarstone Lane
Trimpley Lane
Lost path
Catchems
End

East 5 – Shatterford to Netherton – 4¼ miles

Another way down from the Anglo-Saxon meeting place is to come south as far as the footpath off to Halls Farm (about 1½ miles), but then to stay on the tarmacked road (Trimpley Lane). After avoiding the left-hand turning to Kidderminster and the right-hand turning to Halls Farm, continue down what is now Hoarstone Lane. This is a ridgeway with amazing views to either side, but especially to the west over the valley towards the Severn. You pass Wassell Hill (a very ancient site) on your left. [See Map East 5a] Further on you pass Hoarstone Farm on your right (where there is evidence of occupation in the Roman period) and come down to Trimpley Lane. Here the old route has been lost.

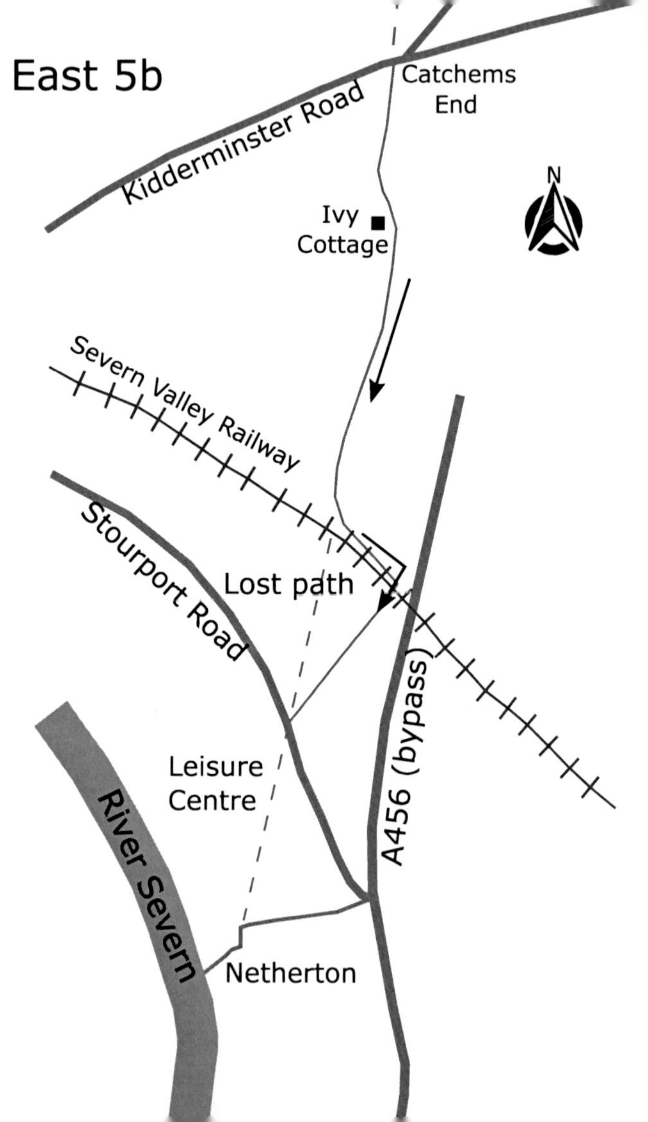

East 5b
Kidderminster Road
Catchems
End
N
Ivy
Cottage
Severn Valley Railway
Stourport Road
Lost path
A456 (bypass)
Leisure
Centre
River Severn
Netherton

It can be seen on a map of 1840 going straight on and coming out at Catchems End. The original driveway up to Warstone House perhaps used it, but none of this is possible as a public footpath now. You will have to continue to the end of Trimpley Lane and turn right down Habberley Road to reach Catchems End. [Move on to Map East 5b]

At Catchems End, carefully cross the road near the Fish & Chip shop and take the lane (on your left as you face Bewdley), passing a couple of cottages on your left (124 and 126 Kidderminster Road). This is called Lodge Banks (though there is no notice to say that) and was originally an access way to Sandbourne House. (It is described going in the other direction in 'Walking Bewdley's History' where it is Walk 11.) The lane leads to Ivy Cottage.

Bear left to follow the trackway up the hill and onto a ridge. Over to your left is the bypass and beyond that is Spring Grove Farm and the West Midlands Safari Park. To your right is the Maypole Piece, which is private land. The ancient route has been interrupted by the railway, so when you reach the track, you have to turn left and then go downhill and turn right under the viaduct to follow the lane down to the main road, the B4195. You pass the site of Sandbourne House; all that remains are the stables, one of the buildings being graced by a clock. There was a house here in the 17th century, so the trackway has long been lost in this area. It probably headed through the area now occupied by the Leisure Centre to reach a crossing of the Severn known as the Guy Head Shoal, somewhere near the end of Netherton Lane.

East 6

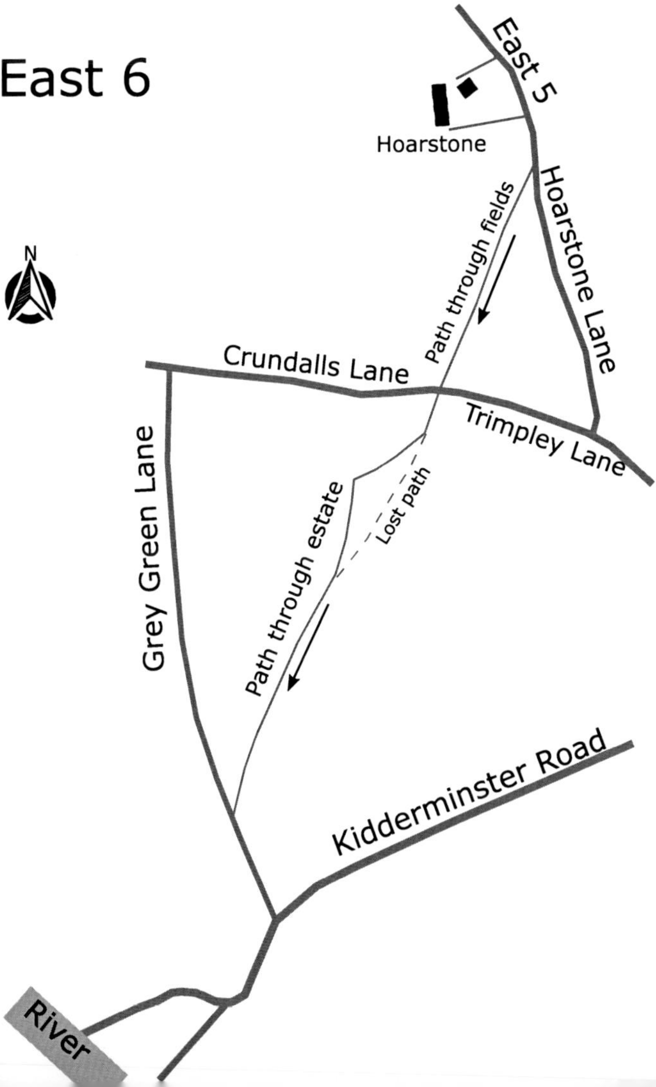

N
East 5
Hoarstone
Hoarstone Lane
Path through fields
Crundalls Lane
Trimpley Lane
Grey Green Lane
Path through estate
Lost path
Kidderminster Road
River

East 6 – Hoarstone to Bewdley – 1 mile

From Hoarstone, there is a way down to Bewdley itself and the old crossing at the Lax Shoal. [See Map East 6]

Coming down from Trimpley, pass the farm on your right and then just past an entrance to Hoarstone Court (the converted barns), also on your right, is a footpath off to the right which goes diagonally across the field to a kissing gate. The path across the next field has a wire fence both sides, so there is a very clear route down to the gate which takes you onto Crundalls Lane. The ancient route has been built upon, but you can walk through the estate to pick it up at the other side.

Cross over into Cordle Marsh Road and follow that (ignoring the turning down Queensway) up to its junction with Shaw

Hedge Road, where you turn left. Follow this road right through to its junction with Damson Way and Spring Hill Rise. On the other side, slightly to your left, is a path, where you can pick up the old route. It goes down past a pylon on your right to meet Grey Green Lane. Turn left to come down to the main Kidderminster Road.

From here, the ancient route probably went down the main road, under the viaduct and bore left to go down Westbourne Street to reach the Stourport Road. A housing development now blocks its way to the Lax Shoal. An alternative in medieval times would have been to continue on the Kidderminster Road right down to the river, where there was a ferry from at least 1300 and a bridge from 1448.

East 7

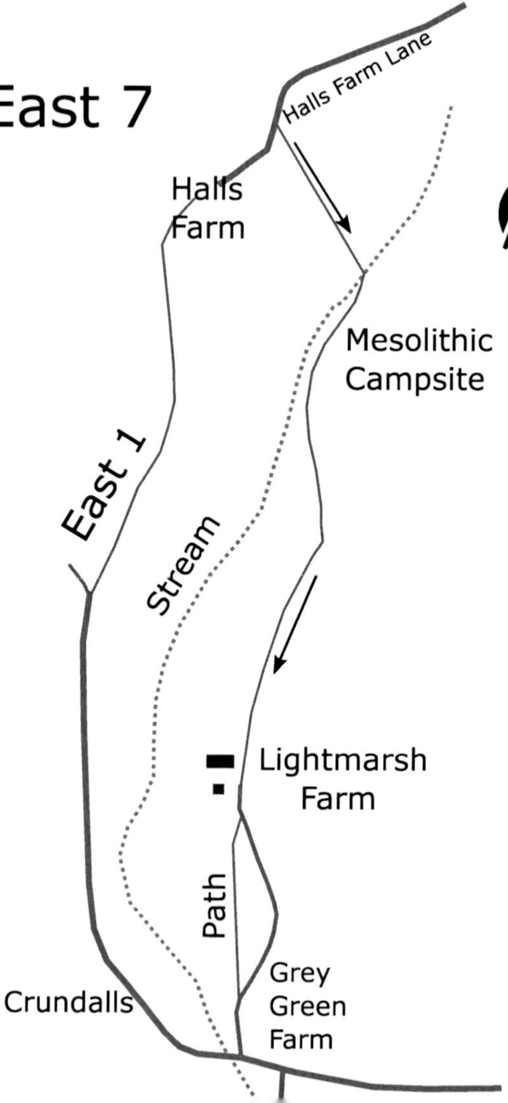
Halls Farm Lane
N
Halls
Farm
Mesolithic
Campsite
East 1
Stream
Lightmarsh
Farm
Path
Grey
Green
Farm
Crundalls

East 7 – Hall's Farm Lane to Bewdley – 2 miles

This route is included because of the archaeological finds in the area. It means there are several ways of coming down from Shatterford to the River Severn. [See Map East 7]

There is a stile to the left of the entrance to The Hawthorns in Hall's Farm Lane. Climb this and keeping the hedge on your right, make for the next stile you can see and into a large open field. The footpath sign tells you to bear slightly right. Walk down into the valley, keeping to the left of the wooden telegraph poles and at the bottom you will find a stream and a couple of planks acting as a footbridge. Cross over the stream, clamber over the stile (not easy) and climb up the bank to follow the path which then turns right and hugs the edge of the field.

It was in this field that evidence of a Mesolithic camp was found when a pipeline was laid in 1992. A total of 1,482 fragments of flint were recovered, mostly comprising waste material but also including 88 artefacts; these are said to be typical of a Later Mesolithic narrow-blade industry. Evidence suggested a temporary site occupied by a small hunting group. Charred hazelnut fragments produced a radiocarbon date of around 8000BC.

The path twists to the right in order to go through a wide opening with a redundant stile on the right-hand side. Look down to your right and you will see the stream a long way down, running through a deep and narrow valley. The best crossing place was probably where the little footbridge was and one can imagine that could have been forded by people long ago. It is, of course, possible that the valley has been deepened by the stream over the years and that prehistoric man was not faced with such a gully.

Once through the opening, continue to hug the hedge on the right until the hedge bends right and it is clear that your path goes straight ahead. Over in the hedge opposite, you will find a modern, metal kissing gate. Go through and turn right, following the hedgeline again right to the bottom of the field where there is an open gate and a broken stile.

Continue to follow the hedgeline and you will come down to a gate where you need to use the stile. A clear track with a wire fence on your left continues downhill to yet another gate, but this one can be opened. You are now in the farmyard of Lightmarsh Farm. There are converted barn buildings to your right and a pond to your left. Walk on along the tarmacked track, past the farmhouse on your right to the point where there is a modern bungalow on your left.

You now have a choice. Over to your right, there is stile leading to a footpath across the field. Ahead of you is the tarmacked road and a wonderful holloway. The holloway would be the ancient route, but it is narrow and the footpath across the field is safer. You have been warned! The footpath joins the road shortly before it comes down onto Crundalls Lane. Grey Green farmhouse is on your left.

Turn left and then quite quickly right to access Grey Green Lane, which will bring you right down into the heart of Bewdley.

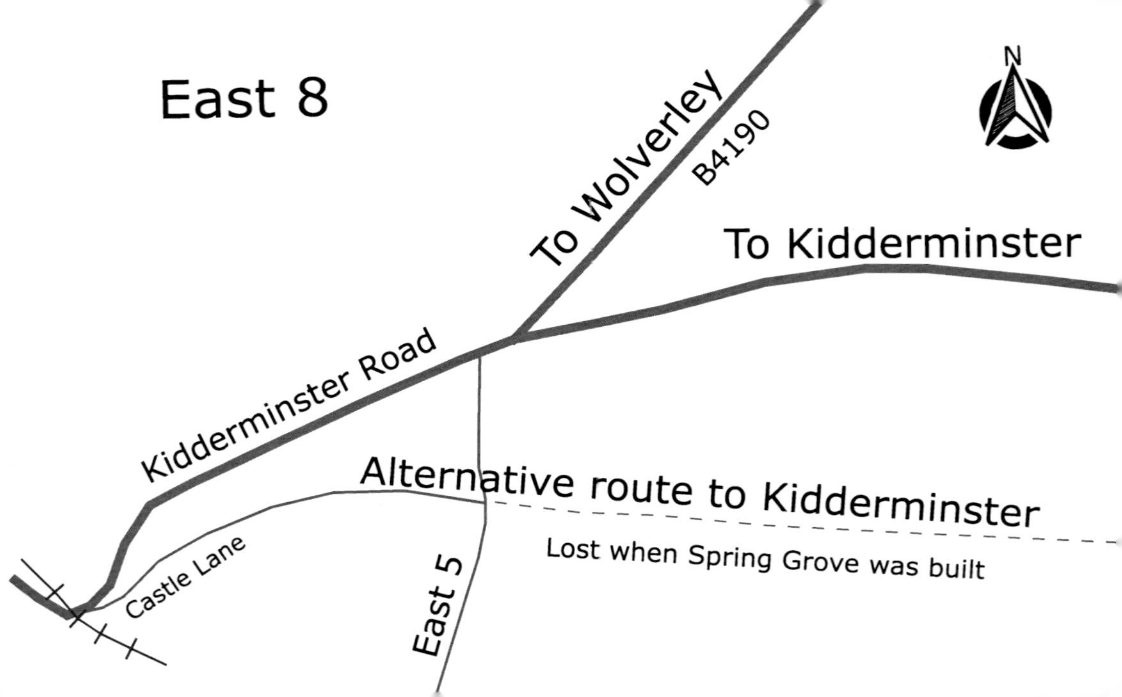
East 8
To Wolverley
B4190
To Kidderminster
Kidderminster Road
Alternative route to Kidderminster
Lost when Spring Grove was built
Castle Lane
East 5
N

East 8 – Two routes to Kidderminster, one now lost

There would have been an ancient trackway between Bewdley and Kidderminster. There seem to have been two, the one being the line of the current main road (the A456) and the other being roughly parallel to this but a bit further south. [See Map East 8]

This second trackway has been almost completely lost, but is known to have existed. In 1771 Francis Best was walking from Caldwell Mill to Bewdley market, but was attacked somewhere near where Spring Grove House would later be built. He was robbed and left to die. His attacker was seen and recognised because he had a club foot – he was John Child and was soon apprehended. We also know that this route was used about the same time by Samuel

Skey on errands he ran between Bewdley and Kidderminster. He so admired the view from Jackystone Hill (as it was then known) that he determined to build a house there; he managed to achieve this some twenty years later. Spring Grove House was completed about 1795.

From Caldwell, the line might have been something like along Greatfield Road and then through Rhydd Covert. Having passed close to Spring Grove House, it must then have crossed over the valley to meet Lodge Banks near Ivy Cottage (see Walk East 5). Old maps show a footpath across the field from Ivy Cottage to the end of Wheatcroft Avenue, but this is not now a public right of way.

The whole of Wheatcroft Avenue would have been the ancient route and then down Castle Lane, but the connection between these two has been broken. Castle Lane joins Kidderminster Road by the Great Western pub.

There would also have been an old route from Wolverley, which is still very clear in the landscape, as it is the B4190 and joins the Kidderminster Road at Catchems End.

Catchems End

The name appears to relate to the boundary between Kidderminster and Wribbenhall and to people being able to avoid the law by crossing the boundary. The name also occurs at Ismere (SO870804) and at Far Forest (SO719760); in both these cases it is a county boundary that is involved.

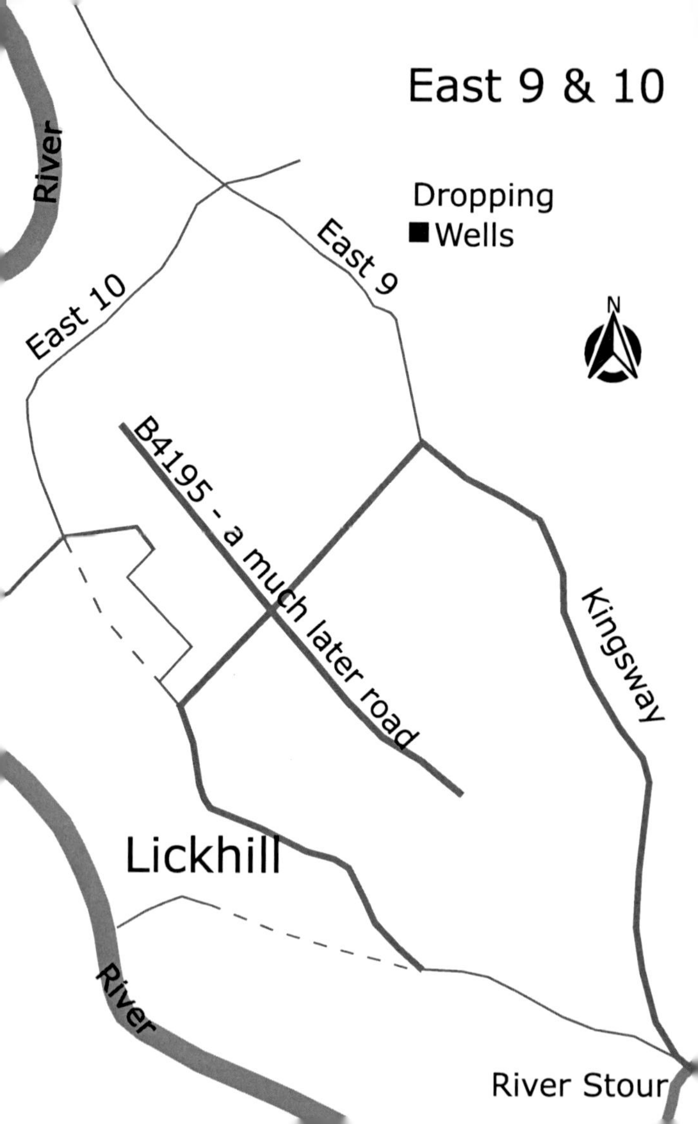
East 9 & 10
Dropping
Wells
N
East 9
East 10
River
B4195 - a much later road
Kingsway
Lickhill
River
River Stour

East 9 – Gilgal to Bewdley via Burlish Top – 3 miles

There were also routes from Stourport; there are two which can be traced as coming from the crossing of the Stour where the current bridge is at the bottom of Gilgal. [See Map East 9 & 10]

One route could have gone almost due north before picking up a trackway roughly on the line of Kingsway. At a left-hand bend in Kingsway, there is a fairly new car park on your right; you join the Geopark Way at this point (see pp. 54-55) and will remain on it until you meet the A456 main road near Blackstone.

Near Burlish, Kingsway makes a sharp left turn (there is a small car park on the right), but the path continues up on to Burlish, [see Map East 9] the pylons being

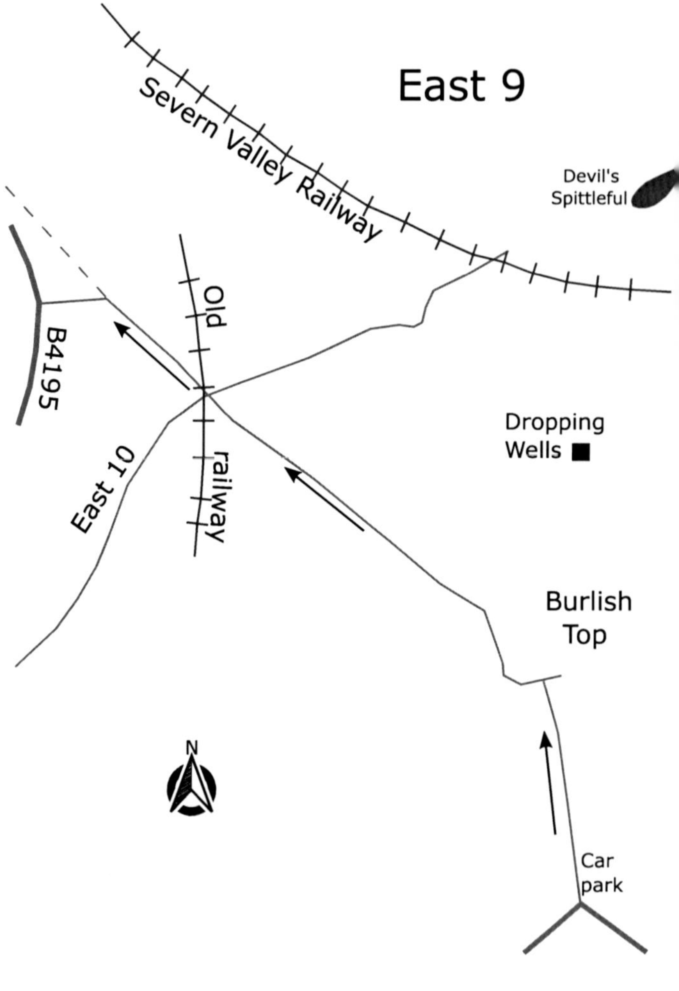
East 9
Severn Valley Railway
Devil's Spittleful
Old railway
B4195
East 10
Dropping Wells
Burlish Top
N
Car park

far over to the right. There is a notice board which advertises the Burlish Top Fitness Trail. There is also a signpost showing left for the Bewdley 45 cycle route and also the Geopark Way. So, turn left and after a short distance the path turns right to go down the hill. Some of it is the cycle route 45, but the footpath also (in places) follows a deep holloway indicative of an ancient route, in use long before the main B4195 was built. In spring there can be clumps of white flowers known as Greater Stitchwort.

You will come down to an unused part of the railway line where it crossed the track via a bridge on its way to Stourport. Go under the bridge and continue straight on along this lane. It is possible that about half way down the lane, the original trackway bore right across the field towards Bewdley.

You meet the main road (the A456) by the old toll house and you are very near to the Guy Head Shoal, so perhaps this was a way that led to this crossing of the Severn. There is from the railway bridge a track going east which takes you past the Devil's Spittleful and might then have continued on to Kidderminster. Perhaps this was a route used by people in Kidderminster wanting to cross the Severn nearer to Ribbesford. There are no obvious routes which lead to such a crossing, but this is a possibility.

East 10 – Gilgal to Bewdley via The Brant – 3¾ miles

Another possible route from Stourport was via Lickhill. From Gilgal, there is a footpath which passes close to Lidl, then down Tan Lane by the Co-op and then past the Primary Academy (on your left) to cross Park Avenue and then diagonally left across the park itself. It can be traced through the housing estate by using Stagborough Way before going down Field End to find a path behind the school which takes you down to the Lickhill Manor Caravan Park. (It is described going in the other direction in "Walking Stourport's History" where it is Walk 6.) There have been some changes here, but there is a shoal at Lickhill, so this path could have led to a crossing of the Severn.

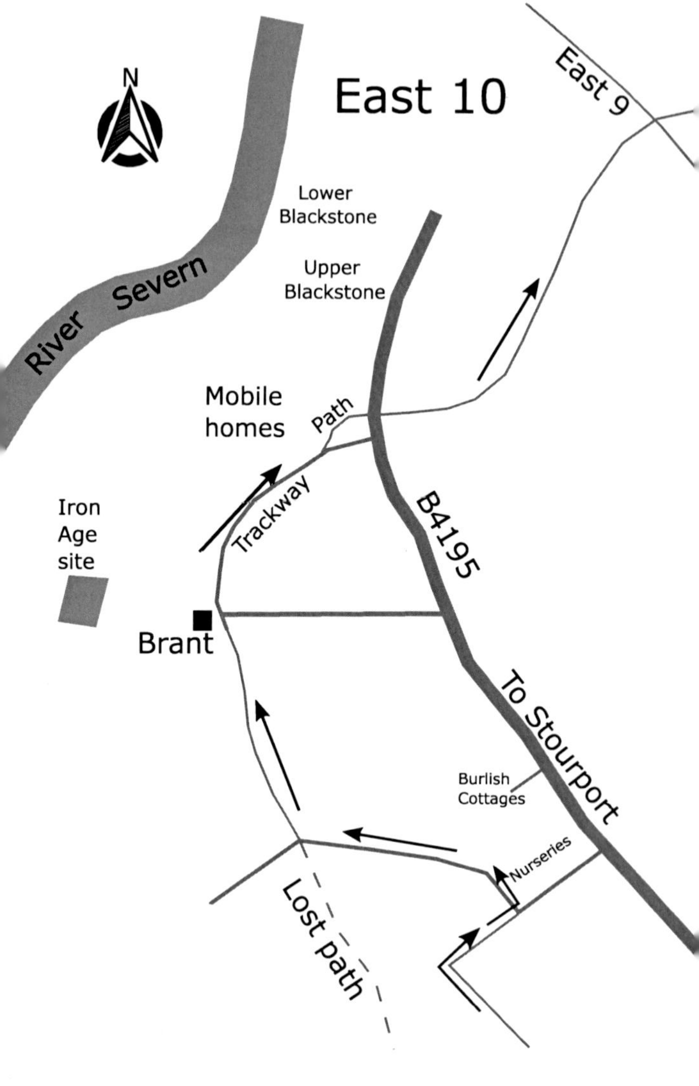
East 10
N
East 9
Lower
Blackstone
Upper
Blackstone
River Severn
Mobile
homes
Path
Trackway
B4195
Iron
Age
site
Brant
To Stourport
Burlish
Cottages
Nurseries
Lost path

There is also a way to come to Bewdley, by ignoring the housing estate and remaining on Lower Lickhill Road until it turns sharply right to go up to the Burlish Crossing traffic lights. There is a track straight ahead, bearing northwest, which goes to Woodgreen Cottages. This is almost certainly an ancient route, but is not completely accessible. Start walking up the track, but after a very short distance you need to climb over the stile on the right. If you get as far as a notice about no access for unauthorised persons, you know you have gone too far!

The path goes along the hedgeline before bending northwest to go up a hill to another stile. Once over the hill, the path goes down into a dip before climbing up the other side to yet another stile. This is a tortuous route. [See Map East 10] You are now in a small pen and need to climb over a stile which is to your right, in the corner. Continue through the field, over another stile and along the fenced in path towards Cook's nursery buildings and once over yet another stile you will find yourself on a concrete driveway. Turn left and follow this. It leads to Severn Bank Caravan Park and to Canine Capers. It turns left and then, as it descends towards the river, you need to turn right to Canine Capers. You are now back on the line of the ancient route.

Walk up this trackway (past Canine Capers on the left) to where it peters out and becomes a pile of rubble and some barbed wire. You have to duck under the barbed wire and hunt for the path on your left. (See the photo on the next page) It is there, complete with broken stile! This is a challenging footpath.

The trackway is still wide, but is VERY overgrown. At the other end, you emerge into the yard of Brant Farm. Just to the west of the Brant (not accessible to the general public) is the site of an Iron Age farmstead, high on the steep hill above the Severn. It is unlikely there was an ancient trackway close to the river; the people of long ago would not have thought the Severn Way was a good route – far too likely to be flooded!

Having the Brant on your left, continue north, towards the caravan park. Where the track turns left at the last mobile home, there is a stile leading to a footpath.

You walk through a deep holloway and out onto the B4195 Stourport road. Carefully cross this busy road to pick up the path on the other side. There is a notice which says it is suitable for carriages, bicycles, horses and people and a second notice which bans cars. Carriages and cars wouldn't stand a chance!

This is a lovely walk. Notice how wide the trackway would have been and look across to your left where you have a view of Wassell Wood House, a white dwelling on the hill in the distance. You may catch a glimpse of the pylons on Burlish Top way over to your right.

Follow the trackway to the disused section of the railway line, where the path meets the route coming down from Burlish (Walk East 9). In ancient times, the traveller could then have turned left to head for Bewdley or could have gone straight over to head for the Devil's Spittleful and Kidderminster.

It is possible that the trackway was used to travel from Kidderminster, via the Devil's Spittleful and the Brant in order to cross the Severn at the Lickhill shoal. It is intriguing that the shoal named after Ribbesford seems not to lead to any trackways, suggesting it was not the main ford. Perhaps the Guy Head shoal was the more used way across the river in this area.

Epilogue

We have offered these routes as possible ancient trackways, but there may well be others.

Edward Thomas in "*The Icknield Way*" wrote: "It is one of the adventurous pleasures of a good map to trace the possible course of a known old road, or to discover one that was lost. A distinct chain of footpath, lane and road … leading across the country and corresponding in much of its course with boundaries is likely to be an ancient way." [quoted in Robert Macfarlane's *The Old Ways*]

We wish you happy hunting and safe walking.

Notes